SCOTTISH DISASTERS
Donald M Fraser

MERCAT PRESS
EDINBURGH

First published in 1996 by Mercat Press
James Thin, 53 South Bridge, Edinburgh EH1 1YS

ISBN 1873644 590

Set in Plantin at Mercat Press
Printed and bound in Great Britain by
Athenæum Press Ltd, Gateshead, Tyne & Wear

For Linda, Marc, Kirsty, Barry, Nikki and Callum Gregor. All of them provided many ideas and good advice, but most of all, prolonged encouragement.

CONTENTS

ILLUSTRATIONS

ACKNOWLEDGEMENTS

Thanks are due to the *Daily Record* for the use of certain photographs. In particular, to Colin MacMillan and Anne Marie Nimmo of that newspaper's Library Department for help and time spent in locating and copying the photographs.

Thanks are also due to David Fowler, Head Librarian, Stornoway Library, Isle of Lewis for the assistance and wealth of material he provided.

Special thanks must be given to Jim Barr, Captain (M.N., Ret.), 'Breona', Nutfield, Australia, who provided much valued technical information and kept me going to the end.

BIOGRAPHY

Donald Fraser was born and brought up in Glasgow. One of his earliest memories—as a three or four-year-old—is of being wakened early every morning by the noise from the boots of thousands of workers as they passed by the tenement houses of Smith Street, Whiteinch, on their way to the many nearby Clyde shipyards. Perhaps his deep interest in the sea, and history, both with a Scottish slant, stems from these early mornings.

Since leaving school in 1969, he has been researching and writing accounts of 'true-life dramas', mainly in his spare time, as he combines his writing with a full-time job. Only in the last five years has he allowed any of his articles to be published in a number of magazines. This is his first book. He is married, with three children, and still lives in Glasgow with his wife, Linda.

He enjoys a good mystery (always with hopes of solving it!) and is always interested to hear of more. He is presently working on his next book, featuring unsolved Scottish mysteries.

FOREWORD

This book deals with Scotland during a bygone era. It was a time before electric light was taken for granted and when fog, of the 'pea soup' variety, could last for a week, unlike the thin mist that persists for a few hours nowadays. Ships did not have radar. Aircraft did not carry fare-paying passengers. All forms of transport were slower, with more serious mechanical failures occurring and certainly without the fancy fail-safe systems prevalent today. Safety regulations were made or amended as and when required. More often than not, this was done in the aftermath of some official inquiry being held, in which faults, ignorance or negligence were identified, but alas too late to help the victims.

Some people might say that these times were hard, although there are those from the present day population who would argue that they were no harder than they are today. One thing is certain though. These were more dangerous times.

This book contains stories of disasters, tragedies and catastrophes, which have almost been lost in time. They include accidents, tales of heroism and, in some instances, of behaviour that was most certainly criminal.

By trial, error and experience, we have reached the stage we are at today. Yet, no matter what precautions we take, accidents will still occur. Hopefully, they will not be of a scale where they can be called disasters, tragedies or catastrophes. Surely, what has occurred before cannot be repeated?

DEATH ON THE CLYDE
A Fatal Ferry Crossing

On the dark winter evening of 30 November 1864, in the heart of Glasgow, a tragedy occurred of a kind never before seen in the city.

That last day of the month had been preceded by three days of torrential rain, sleet and snow. The river Clyde, which gives the city its north/south divide, was in spate, with a chill winter wind blowing. Even so, the population was going about its business without too much interruption.

In those far off days, Glasgow did not have the proliferation of bridges spanning the Clyde that it now enjoys. In order to cross the river, it was necessary to use one of the many small ferries that were situated at the foot of some of the city's streets that led down to the riverbank. The Clyde Street Ferry was one of them. Reached by stairs descending from street level, the ferry was no more than a large broad rowing boat. Owned and operated by the River Clyde Trust, it was licensed to carry 24 passengers plus a crew of one.

Each ferry was normally in the charge of one man, who could be on duty for ten or twelve hours at a time. The man in command of the vessel that evening was John Rodger, a 23-year-old assistant ferryman who had held the job for five months. He had been on duty for most of that day, a day on which the weather had started with sleet and snow, turning eventually to incessant rain. Only the strong wind that was still blowing had been a constant element that day.

With the excessive number of hours worked by the ferrymen, even the fittest of men needed a rest from the continuous strain of rowing passengers back and forth across the river. Occasionally, when a passenger volunteered to row the ferry for a particular journey, in lieu of

1

payment of the fare, the offer was gladly accepted, and a much-needed break from routine was taken. This was a practice the owners were fully aware of, but to which they turned a blind eye.

About five minutes after six that evening, the ferryboat was moored on the north bank of the river, at the stairs adjacent to Clyde Street, awaiting its usual complement of workers. With the nearby factories and warehouses finishing work for the day at 6 p.m., many of the employees used the ferry to cross the river on the way to their homes in the south side of the city.

As the passengers were clambering aboard, the paddle steamer *Inveraray Castle* passed by slowly on her way upriver to her berth. The ferry quickly filled up with workmen and boarding was soon refused to a number of other intending passengers. As it moved away from the quay, rowed by a willing passenger, most of the men were standing up in the vessel. The boat had no covering to protect it from the weather, and as a result, all the seats were soaking wet. No one wanted to sit in those conditions, although it was only a short crossing.

The little vessel had barely reached midway when disaster struck. It was swamped by a large wave, which came right over her gunwale and half flooded the vessel with river water. The ferocity and suddenness of the wave caused an oar to be torn from the grasp of the rower. This in turn caused the ferry to rock violently from side to side. As the majority of passengers were standing, they overbalanced, pitching the boat even further. At this point, some of the occupants either jumped or were involuntarily thrown overboard into the ice-cold river. Almost immediately, the ferry was struck by another large wave, which sealed its fate. The boat heeled over to its port side and the remaining workers were catapulted into the stormy waters.

Some of the passengers began swimming towards the north bank of the river, from where they had set out, as it was the nearer. Others found that the ferry had not sunk, but had turned bottom up and they managed to grab hold of it before it was swept away from the scene by the fast running currents.

The ferry on the opposite shore heard the cries for help from the passengers now in the water, and immediately set out to assist. On reaching the middle of the river, it could find no trace of either passengers or vessel.

Those same shouts had also carried to the north bank, and in particular to River Police Constable Gavin Livingstone, who instructed the crew of the steamer *Celt*, berthed nearby, to launch a rescue boat from the ship. The crew could not find anyone in the water, but continued to hear cries and found them coming from the overturned ferry with four workmen clinging to its sides. They followed the wreck as it was swept downriver, all the time looking for a suitable opportunity to effect the rescue of the passengers.

By this time, some of the stronger swimmers amongst the passengers were reaching the safety of the quayside. A large crowd had gathered, some alerted by the shouts of those in the water, while others had merely been queuing for the return of the ferry for the next journey. A man named Gibb had almost reached the bank when he was spotted by the crowd, who, seeing that he was exhausted, threw planks of wood into the water. Fortunately, the barrage of well intentioned missiles missed him, but Gibb was too weak to reach out for them.

On seeing this, another member of the River Police, Constable Alexander Campbell, took a hand in the matter. By standing on the stairs below the water line, he managed to grab hold of Gibb with a life-hook, and with further assistance from two members of the crowd, pulled him from the river and to safety. Gibb was taken immediately to a nearby hotel, where he received medical attention, recovering quickly enough from his ordeal to walk home.

Another survivor, David Hill, climbed from the river unaided but exhausted, and was taken to the River Police Office a short distance away. He was examined by the on-duty police surgeon, and after regaining his stamina, Hill thanked the doctor, left the office and walked home.

James Stewart was a good swimmer and he managed to reach the side of a vessel on the north bank, where he hung onto a small boat attached to its side. His cries for help went unnoticed and, after a short rest, he then struck out for the quayside. Before he could reach it, he was spotted by the crowd, now on the lookout for any sign of movement in the darkness, and hauled onto dry land. Stewart declined any medical attention, gave his name and address to the police at the scene, and made his way home.

By now, the upturned vessel was reaching the area of the Hydepark Street Ferry, about 300 yards south of Clyde Street. The shouts of the passengers hanging onto the boat were heard by Dugald Cochrane, ferryman in charge of the Hydepark boat. In the darkness, Cochrane began to manoeuvre his ferry towards the cries. Within a minute, he had located the ferry and found three men hanging onto the keel, whilst another was clinging for his life to the gunwale of the stricken vessel. Along with the crew of the small boat from the *Celt*, Cochrane was able to rescue all four passengers quickly and then bring them safely to shore at Hydepark Street.

Two of those saved quietly thanked their rescuers and disappeared into the night without giving their names. Another, Robert Wilson, recovered and walked home in the company of a policeman. The fourth man rescued, John Kane, was found to be unconscious and taken in that condition to the police office. He came to after the attentions of the police doctor and was sent to his home in a cab, arriving there about 8 p.m. On seeing his wife, his first words to her were, 'I'm dying'. He began coughing and vomiting blood and was helped to his bed but died within the hour.

News of the tragedy had spread very quickly to all corners of the city and the office of the River Police was beseiged with callers. A list of people, numbering about 35, who were thought to have been involved in the tragedy, was compiled from worried relatives who had called at the office.

The chief of police, Captain McFarlane, asked for assistance from Humane Society House in providing boats and men to begin a search of the river. A similar call was made to Renfrew Police. A Mr Geddes of the Humane Society attended immediately and began dragging the murky depths of the swollen river in the area around Clyde Street, but he could not find any trace of those who had perished.

Because of the weather and the darkness, the search was called off for the night at 10 p.m., with the intention of resuming it at first light the following morning. Then, when all hope had been abandoned of finding any more survivors, George Buchanan was brought to the scene of the tragedy. He had been a passenger, who, on swimming to a large steamer moored on the north bank, only had the strength to pull himself from the water into a small boat next to the steamer. He was eventually seen by the crew of the larger vessel and rescued. After he recovered, he returned to the scene, gave his account of the incident and was walked to his home by a policeman.

The following day at 8 a.m. sharp, the search for the victims resumed with six boats. Two were crewed by staff of the Humane Society whilst the other four were filled by men from the Clyde Trust. The area to be searched was confined to that stretch of the river between Clyde Street and Hydepark Street.

At the beginning of the search, the list of the men reported missing that was held by the police had almost halved since the previous night. Some of those whose names had appeared on the list had gone straight from work to enjoy a night out, while others merely arrived home

4

later than usual. Relieved relatives were more than happy to return to the police office to have the names deleted from the record.

Large crowds had formed on both banks of the river and included a number of relatives of the missing men. Each time a grappling hook was thrown into the water, a hush came over the spectators, and with every empty pull of the hook to the surface, the crowd would collectively murmur with disappointment.

Within two hours of the beginning of the search, the first body was recovered. From then until 5 p.m., a total of 17 bodies were reclaimed from the bottom of the river in this area. The bodies were landed on the south bank and thereafter some were taken to a nearby shed at the Clyde Trust's yard and others to Receiving House at Windmillcraft. Relatives of the missing men made their way to the makeshift mortuaries, and after identifying their loved ones, had their bodies removed in order to make funeral arrangements.

After the rescue of the four men who had clung to the upturned ferry, the boat had been forgotten about and was allowed to drift away. It was found the day following the tragedy at Stobcross Quay, further down the Clyde, undamaged.

By now, the details of the tragedy were becoming clearer. Twenty-seven people had been aboard the little ferry on her fateful trip. Nineteen had drowned, whilst another, John Kane, had died as a result of the tragedy. Sixteen of those who perished were youths or men aged between 17 and 26 years of age, with the majority of them being unmarried.

For the next week, the river was dragged daily for the two remaining victims. Despite searches going on from 8 a.m. until 10 p.m., and ships berthed at the quayside at the time of the incident being moved from their moorings to facilitate a thorough search, no trace could be found of them. One body was recovered during this period, but it was later confirmed that this person was unconnected with the ferry sinking. It was not until ten days after the tragedy that the last two bodies were recovered.

An Inquiry into the disaster was immediately called for, but prior to one being set up, the Ferries Commission of the Clyde Trust met on 5 December to discuss the tragedy and its probable causes. The passing of the paddle steamer *Inveraray Castle* minutes before the ferry sailed was considered to be a main cause. The wash from its paddles was blamed for the large waves that swept over the little boat. No matter that the steamer's captain gave evidence later at the official Inquiry that he had observed the ferry at the stairs and that on passing it he was going dead slow. It was discovered that the paddles on the vessel were of an older, non-feathered type which were known to cause a larger than normal wash.

Also taken into consideration were the facts known about the weather on the evening and the resultant state of the river. Another factor was that an inexperienced passenger was rowing the vessel, which was captained by a relatively new ferryman who had certainly overloaded the ferry with too many people and had allowed the majority of them to stand during the crossing of the turbulent river.

What was not considered, and ought to have been, is the type of clothing worn by the passengers. With the weather so cold, large overcoats on top of jackets, overalls on top of trousers and heavy working men's boots would have been their normal attire. Trying to swim in a river wearing all, or even some, of that type of clothing would have been almost impossible.

The one piece of good news to come out of the tragedy was that the public outcry that followed forced the Clyde Trust to place an order with the shipbuilding yard of Hedderwicks at Govan for a modern, and safer, steam-engined ferry to replace the rowing boat at Clyde Street. The vessel came into service the following year and within a short space of time all of the Trust-operated ferries changed over to this new style ferry.

The river was to be the scene of one last tragic act. On the day following the Commission's meeting, while the search was continuing for the bodies of the final two victims, a member of the search party fell overboard from one of the boats and was swept away and drowned.

Tragedies on the river had happened before and would happen again. Fortunately, in these later incidents, not one ferry was involved. A hard lesson had been learned.

A KILLER WIND
The Lost Eyemouth Fishing Fleet

Scotland's weather has long been a topic of conversation. Never a day passes without some comment about that over which we have no control.

Although this country is considered to have a moderate climate, it still suffers occasionally from extreme weather. Within living memory, the great blizzards of 1947 and 1963 and the mighty gale of 1968 all spring to mind. Similar conditions were experienced in October 1881, when a great hurricane blew across Scotland and left behind a trail of destruction never seen before or since.

The week had started quietly for the fishermen of the town of Eyemouth on Scotland's east coast. The herring season had been over for a month and the nets normally used to catch them were being repaired before being stored away to await the new season. At the same time as repairing the nets, the men were making up fishing lines, as they would be needed later that week when the boats would be going to sea, hoping to catch haddock and other white fish.

The Eyemouth fleet totalled 45 boats, all but four of them being large deep-sea vessels. These larger boats normally carried a crew of seven, whereas the smaller ones, or yawls as they were called, had space for only four men.

Friday morning, 15 October 1881, dawned with a bright blue cloudless sky and only the gentlest of breezes. About half a mile outside the town's harbour is a group of rocks protruding above the surface of the sea and known as 'the Hurcars'. In any weather, the waves always break over the rocks, giving an area of white surf, but that morning, beyond the rocky outcrop, the water was only occasionally speckled with foam.

As the men readied their vessels for a day's fishing it was noticed that the reading on the barometer on the end of the harbour wall had changed from 'Fine' to 'Stormy Weather' and that the pressure was now showing 27", which was the lowest ever recorded in the town. The harbour master ran the storm warning flag up the mast and brought these facts to the attention of the fishermen. However, due to the fleet having lain idle all week, which meant that the crews had not earned any money, and with shoals of fish known to be close to the shore, the fishermen decided to put to sea, trusting their ability to read the sky and the sea better than any barometer.

As there was hardly any wind that fine morning, the brown coloured sails, the trademark of the Eyemouth fleet, hung limp. The boats were rowed by the crews until they had cleared the Hurcars and the shelter of the bay where they found that there was enough of a breeze for the sails to take over.

By 8 a.m. that morning, the harbour was empty. All 45 vessels were making for the fishing grounds, which lay between six and ten miles from the shore. For one vessel, the *Press Home,* it was a special occasion. She had only been delivered from the builders the night before and now it was on her maiden voyage.

On reaching the fishing grounds the crews cast their lines and fished quietly until just before noon, when dark clouds quickly came rolling in from the east, completely covering the sky and the sun. The darkness was such that it was impossible for one boat to see the nearest boat to it. A crew member later remarked that the darkness came upon the fleet 'like the clap of a hand'.

Then came the roaring hurricane winds, whipping the sea up before it in a frenzy. Some boats managed to take in their lines, whilst others deliberately cut them as the fleet attempted to run for shelter. The fierce winds tore the sails of almost every vessel to shreds. The boats were tossed about as if they were toys while waves broke over the vessels, sending a spray of salt water to drench the crews. The howling wind forced the accompanying rain and hail hard into the faces of the crews, stinging them with a pain, the ferocity of which they had never experienced. The mountainous seas split the fleet into two groups. Some of the vessels were forced towards the shore while others were pushed farther out to sea.

Back on land, the severity of the storm meant that the school children of Eyemouth had to be sent home from lessons, while houses and shops were left empty as the people, worried about the fleet, hurriedly made their way to the harbour. The crowds waited, braving the torrential rain and ferocious wind for almost two hours before the first vessels came into sight. Three boats were spotted and the spectators were tense as they watched them battle with the huge seas. With every minute that passed, the vessels were getting a little closer to the harbour.

As they entered the safe haven, it was noticed that they were not part of the Eyemouth fleet, but yawls from Coldingham Shore, a village further south along the coast. Nonetheless, their crews were given a warm welcome.

Next to come into view was an Eyemouth boat, the *Onward*. She fought her way to safety, but not without cost, as she had lost one of her crew, the captain's son, who had been swept overboard as they had neared land. Two more of the Eyemouth fleet, the *Alabama* and the *Britannia* arrived at the harbour safely, with only the damage to their sails to show for their struggles.

Just before 3 p.m. two more boats from Coldingham arrived at the pier, and their crews were pulled onto land, safe but exhausted. Just as this was happening, the spectators observed another Eyemouth boat, the *Harmony*, a few hundred yards away. The vessel was fighting hard against the elements. She was forcing her way through the heavy surf, occasionally disappearing from view. As she reached the entrance to the harbour, she was lifted up by a large wave, which seemed to want to sweep the boat into the haven. As the vessel sat atop the crest of the wave, another, larger, wave rose up behind the *Harmony* and crashed down onto her, smashing her to pieces. Not one of the seven crew was seen again. Although it had happened close to them, none of the crowd could offer any assistance due to the appalling weather.

Word of the *Harmony*'s fate spread quickly through the town, as men, on their way to bring life-saving apparatus from a shed a half mile away from the harbour, related the story. By the time the men returned with the equipment over a thousand people, a third of the town's population, had gathered in the harbour area. The crowds stood in silence, numbed by what they had just witnessed. Just then, another vessel, the *Radiant*, loomed out of the darkness, on the same course as the ill-fated *Harmony*.

The *Radiant* battled the raging seas and was about ten yards from the harbour entrance when a tremendous gust of wind, much stronger than previous ones, blew across the bay. A large wave bore down on the vessel and smashed her against the rocks at the side of the harbour walls, breaking her into pieces. Desperate to make some effort, the crowd threw ropes which, although weighted with stones, were blown back over their heads.

The crew were seen struggling in the foaming water, their cries and screams mixing with those on shore. One man was observed trying to swim towards the rocks, but because of the waves, he could not climb onto them. A number of men from the harbour formed a human chain in an effort to reach him and they got close enough to speak to him, with the last man even briefly touching the swimmer's hand. Just then, a wave brought a broken piece of the *Radiant* down on top of the swimmer and he sank out of sight, like the rest of the crew, never to resurface.

As this episode was being played out, yet another vessel loomed out of the darkness and into sight. The crowd quickly identified her as the *Press Home*, as she was the only one in the fleet to bear white-coloured sails. So new was she, she had not yet had her name painted on her bows. As the vessel steered for home, a giant wave struck her, turning her upside down. Through the rolling waves, some of her crew could be seen climbing on top of the upturned boat, but a moment later she was struck by another huge wave and both vessel and crew disappeared beneath the seething waters.

All the men perished, but still the storm had not finished with the *Press Home*, as a minute later, she rose from the depths and was smashed to smithereens on the rocks. The wife of one of the crew members was led away in anguish. They had been married for only a week!

The *Pilgrim*, of the Eyemouth fleet, had been directly behind the *Press Home*, on an identical course. She had been caught up in the same waves as the preceding vessel and looked likely to suffer a similar fate as she was forced towards the rocks. The *Pilgrim* disappeared from sight in the trough of a tremendous wave and the spectators gave up all hope for her safety. As the sea ebbed, the crowd saw the *Pilgrim* lying in the smooth waters between the shore and some rocks. The wave had lifted her clear of the danger and the craft was undamaged. Lines were thrown to the vessel and the crew were landed safely.

What was happening at Eyemouth was being repeated at other harbours on the east coast. At Burnmouth, a small fishing port about four miles east of Eyemouth, locals gathered at the harbour to await the return of their small fleet of vessels. Apart from two cobbles (small boats) belonging to their own village, the first large vessel to reach Burnmouth was the *Janet*, from Eyemouth. Two hundred yards from shore, she struck a group of rocks known as the 'Carrs' with the loss of all her crew.

About twenty minutes later, the *Lily Of The Valley* was seen making her way toward Burnmouth's haven. Not far from the entrance the vessel was struck by a large wave which capsized her. Her crew were never seen again. Both boats were carried away on huge waves and smashed to pieces on the rocks. Three more Eyemouth vessels, the *James and Robert*, the *Sweet Home* and the *Brothers*, were all driven onto the rocks, but their crews were rescued by some Burnmouth villagers who were bravely manning small boats.

As night fell on the fishing port it became clear that of the 45 boats that put to sea, only seven had been accounted for. Lights burned in almost every house in the town, as hardly a home was unaffected by the day's events. Relatives of the fathers, sons or brothers still missing sat up all night, waiting for word and praying for the safe return of their loved ones.

The next day, Saturday, brought no relief to the population of Eyemouth. Some of the relatives had hoped that the fleet had sailed further out to sea in an effort to ride out the storm, which in turn meant that it would take longer for the vessels to return to their home port. Their hopes were dashed when news began filtering through from other ports along the coast of wreckage and bodies being washed ashore.

Later that day, reports were collated from the surrounding areas which showed that twenty vessels, thirteen of them from Eyemouth, were confirmed as sunk, with the loss of ninety-four men. The small port of Cove was particularly affected. Twenty-one men from the village had put to sea that fateful morning, but only ten had returned. Cove had lost more than half of its fishermen in a single day.

Early on Sunday morning, word spread around the town that a boat was approaching the harbour. In minutes, the harbour walls were crammed with townsfolk, eager to catch a glimpse of the vessel. Very soon, the boat was identified as the *Ariel Gazelle* and she slowly steered herself into port. Relatives mobbed the exhausted crew. One more vessel from the fleet also arrived later that day. The *Economy* limped into harbour without her captain, who had been washed overboard during the hurricane.

During that day, more survivors arrived in Eyemouth, but not by boat. The crew from the *White Star* arrived from North Shields, while the men from the *Enterprise* had travelled from Berwick, sadly minus one who had perished. Just before midnight, the crew of the *Fisher Lassies* arrived in the town, having walked from the railway station in nearby Burnmouth. They had managed to berth their vessel in South

11

Shields. By now, 11 boats and 71 men were still missing. As each crew or vessel returned, the elation of the relatives was tempered by the sorrow of those other townfolk whose hopes had been dashed, when they realised that their loved ones were not among the survivors.

The following two days saw a number of funerals taking place in Eyemouth. The only people not to attend the services were those whose loved ones were still missing. They were out searching the shoreline in an attempt to find any trace of their relatives.

By Wednesday all hope for any more survivors had vanished. The final count revealed that the hurricane had claimed the lives of 189 fishermen from the east coast, 129 of them from Eyemouth alone. Only 30 bodies were ever recovered.

A Disaster Fund was immediately set up. Cities, towns and villages the length and breadth of Scotland, and England too, all sent donations. £100 was sent from the fund of the Tay Bridge Disaster, which had occurred only two years earlier. Queen Victoria also sent a donation. Within two weeks, £54,000 had been received into the fund. It was enough to provide a weekly income for the 73 widows for the rest of their lives, during which time they had to bring up the 263 fatherless children left as a result of the great storm.

FROM SLIPWAY TO
SHIPWRECK
The Doomed SS Daphne

The morning of Tuesday 3 July, 1883 dawned bright and sunny and the men and boys of the workforce of shipbuilders Alexander Stephen and Son, of Linthouse, Glasgow, were in high spirits.

The reasons for these good feelings were two-fold. The Glasgow Fair holidays were fast approaching and another Clyde-built ship was due to be launched that morning. The order books of the shipyard were full, as indeed were those of the other Clyde shipyards, for this was during the heyday of shipbuilding. If further proof were needed of this fact, Stephen's yard had six berthing docks, which were fully occupied by vessels in various stages of completion.

The ship being launched that day, the steamship SS *Daphne*, had been commissioned by the firm A A Laird and Co., for use by their subsidiary, the Glasgow and Londonderry Steam Packet Company Ltd. The *Daphne* was intended for use in coastal waters, carrying passengers and livestock between Northern Ireland and Glasgow. She was not a particularly large ship, weighing only 500 tons deadweight and 175 feet in length. Stephens had previously built vessels five times heavier and twice as long. It was intended that the ship be ready and sailing this route by the following Thursday (12 July) for the start of the traditional Fair holidays.

About 11.25 a.m., five minutes before high tide on the river, the naming ceremony began. John Stephen, yard superintendent and later to become managing director of the shipyard, was in charge of the launch. Aboard the *Daphne* at this time were squads of tradesmen

Rescue operations ongoing as the tide ebbs, exposing more of the hull of SS Daphne. *Inset: John Stephen, yard superintendent.* (Mitchell Library)

numbering almost two hundred. Plumbers, carpenters, engineers, boilermen and apprentices of all trades, were busy working away at their various jobs, the majority of them below decks, oblivious to what was going on ashore.

Because of the approaching holidays, when the shipyards would close for two weeks, and the fact that the SS *Daphne* would be required to be completed and handed over to her new owners prior to those holidays, the vessel was being launched in a rush, with only her engines fitted. Added to this, an unusually large amount of timber, needed by the carpenters on board to put the finishing touches to the ship, had been stacked high on the main deck.

The intention was to launch the *Daphne* in this incomplete state and afterwards tow her to a berth at the nearby Broomielaw, where her boilers and all other furnishings would be fitted. However, the management of Stephens considered that the time taken up by the launch and subsequent towing of the ship upriver, coupled with the fact that the tradesmen would have to make their own way from the yard to the Broomielaw, would result in the loss of a much needed half a day of worktime. The company's idea of putting the workmen aboard prior to the launch, allowing them to work continuously on the vessel, made good business sense to them.

In those halcyon days of shipbuilding, Glaswegians had been brought up on a steady diet of launches, and as the SS *Daphne* was not considered anything out of the ordinary, only a few hundred spectators had gathered on the river's edges to view the proceedings.

At exactly 11.30 a.m., the SS *Daphne* began sliding down the tallow-encrusted slipway, towards the first taste of water on her metal. As she entered the river stern-first, she appeared to go very deep into the fast-running tide, followed almost immediately by a heavy lurch to her port side. At this point, some of the men working on deck, veterans of numerous launchings and fearing what was to come next, leapt from the vessel and into the river.

The *Daphne* momentarily swung back towards starboard in an effort to right herself, quivered and then toppled over onto her port side and sank immediately. Many of the men who had jumped into the water at the first sign of disaster did not have time to swim away and were trapped or crushed as the vessel came down on top of then. Some others, including the lucky ones thrown from the ship into the river, were managing to cling to wooden debris, which moments before had been stacked aboard the ship. They were frantically trying to avoid being sucked into the huge vortex caused by the sinking ship. The rapidity of the sinking was mainly due to the fact that the hatches for the livestock cargo holds had not yet been made and fitted, which allowed torrents of water into the hull of the ship.

The *Daphne* eventually settled on the bottom of the river, almost midway between the two banks, and, unbelievably, some survivors were able to await rescue by standing on her hull, as it was only a few feet below the surface.

The crowd of spectators had been numbed by the horror they had just witnessed, but quickly came to their senses and began throwing anything that would float into the water to assist those struggling to survive. Five small rowing boats from the shipyard of Barclay, Curle and Co. of Partick, whose yard was opposite that of Stephens, were crewed and launched into the river. Between them, the boats managed to rescue ten men from drowning. An unknown plater from the same yard twice dived into the river and saved a workman on each occasion. He was prevented from entering the waters a third time by fellow workers, as by now, he himself was exhausted. Of the great number of survivors pulled from the disaster, only one required any medical treatment.

After an hour, the only visible signs of tragedy were the many small boats at the site and the silence of the crowds of onlookers. Word had soon spread of the disaster and the crowds were quickly becoming larger on both sides of the river. Relatives and friends of the workmen still trapped in the sunken hull of the *Daphne* had come from their nearby homes in both the Govan and Partick districts of Glasgow to see the full horror for themselves.

By 2 p.m. divers had been summoned and the tide was now ebbing. The starboard side of the *Daphne* was visible above the surface and the crowds had increased to thousands. Two bodies had been recovered and quickly removed to a shed within the yard that had been set up as a makeshift mortuary. Wooden walkways around the yard that afforded a view of the river were crowded with spectators. Fears were expressed that the walkways might collapse with the sheer weight of numbers of the onlookers, throwing more people into the river at the site of the disaster. Extra police were summoned, and together with members of Stephens' workforce, they successfully cleared the walkways and the danger. A police guard was mounted to prevent any further encroachment.

By 4 p.m., the divers who had been sent for were hard at work and had recovered nine more bodies, this time from inside the stricken vessel. The divers had reported that the interior of the ship was unusually warm and that they had seen more victims within the various compartments, many still holding the tools of their trade in their hands, so quickly had they been overcome by events. Unfortunately many of these compartments had small entrances, and the divers could not gain access to them, for fear of entangling their air tubes, for these were the days of diving suits with large metal helmets. The rescue operations were kept going overnight and a small boat was moored over the sunken ship to warn other river traffic of the danger.

First newspaper reports of the catastrophe stated that 150 lives were feared lost, while 50 men were either rescued or had swum ashore, in the Clyde's worst ever disaster. Within twenty-four hours, a list with the names of the missing men was published. Alongside this list was another, with the names of the men whose bodies had been recovered. Day after day, the list of missing grew shorter at the expense of the list of recoveries. Six of those who perished were apprentices aged only 14 and 15 years old.

A Disaster Fund was immediately set up, with the hope of raising at least £50,000.

Survivors gave interviews and spoke of their immediate fears when the *Daphne* was going down the slipway. They considered that she went down faster than was normal, which in turn caused the vessel to enter the river deeper than usual for a ship of her size. Some also expressed grave doubts about the wisdom of having large amounts of timber piled high on deck, and coupled with the fact that she only had her engines fitted, they now believed, with hindsight, that the SS *Daphne*'s centre of gravity was far too high.

A factor that also contributed to the disaster, and something of which the survivors would have been unaware at the time of their interviews, was that the drag chains and anchors attached to the vessel, meant to be a means of slowing the descent down the slipway and onwards into the river, did not work properly. The port anchor was dragged a distance of 20 yards, whilst for some unexplained reason, the starboard anchor only travelled six yards. Some reports of the tragedy have stated that the port anchor went as far as 60 yards.

What we can be sure of is the fact that when the *Daphne* entered the river, uneven tensions were being applied to her. This, added to her centre of gravity being higher than normal, meant that when she listed to her port side, the list could not be corrected and she finally toppled over.

The day after the disaster, the Lord Provost of Glasgow received a telegram from Sir Henry Ponsonby on behalf of Queen Victoria, which read: 'The Queen hopes that the acccount of the loss of life at the launch on the Clyde is exaggerated. Her Majesty, who is deeply grieved at the disaster, asks if you can give her any further information.' A reply was immediately dispatched to Buckingham Palace informing her of all that had happened and what was now being done in the aftermath.

By Thursday 5 July, divers had recovered 52 bodies, all of which had been identified by grieving relatives as soon as they had been laid out in the makeshift mortuary. Many of the dead were immediately removed and taken to their homes. Stephens had informed relatives that the company would bear the costs of all funeral expenses.

By this date, the Disaster Fund that had been set up was receiving money from street collections that had been held all over the city. Many factories made collections from the shop floor and sent these to the fund. Even Queen Victoria made a donation, sending a personal cheque for £100. In the first week alone, over £17,000 was raised, which in those days was a phenomenal sum.

The rescue operation went on for the next two weeks, and over 5,000 spectators gathered on both banks of the river each day to watch over the proceedings. Two teams of divers were now working round

Sir Edward Reed, MP, who led the inquiry into the Daphne *disaster.*
(Mitchell Library)

the clock, along with salvage experts. One team spent their time trying to locate more of the dead, while the other team were making preparations to raise the *Daphne* from the river bed. This operation was being impeded by the amount of river traffic passing the site, as by now the annual holidays had started. The exodus of Glaswegians on trips 'doon the watter' meant that ships of all shapes and sizes were passing the scene every five or ten minutes.

Bodies were being recovered on a daily basis and by Friday 20 July, 116 dead had been recovered from the vessel. On this day, the salvage team were successful in refloating the *Daphne*, after which the final eight bodies were located and removed from its interior. The stricken vessel was then towed upriver and berthed at the Broomielaw to await her fate.

By now, people were beginning to ask questions about the cause of the catastrophe, and blame was being apportioned, without proof, to everyone from the then unknown designer of the *Daphne*, to Stephens the builders, and to a lesser extent, the yard workforce. It was decided that a full inquiry into the disaster should be held, and when it convened under the chairmanship of Sir Edward Reed, MP, at the Court House in Glasgow, it took evidence from everyone concerned.

The Inquiry issued a report, some 73 pages long, a short time later. Its findings, made public, completely exonerated everyone remotely connected with the disaster, concluding that it had been an appalling accident that could not have been foreseen.

The Disaster Fund reached a total of £30,000 and was controlled by leading Glasgow City dignitaries of the day. All the money collected was paid out to relatives, some of whom were now in dire financial straits, due to having lost the breadwinner of their family in the disaster.

The *Daphne* was later completely refitted and handed over to her owners, who wisely renamed her SS *Rose*. For many years she plied the Irish Channel between Ireland and Scotland, and many times, on journeys to Glasgow, passed the site of her sinking that became the temporary grave of 124 men and boys.

POISON IN THE QUARRY
The Day Trip that Turned to Tragedy

In 1886, Glasgow was in the middle of a massive rebuilding programme. A new, purpose-built City Chambers had earlier been commissioned and was now in the process of being erected. Large areas of the city were either being repaired or replaced. Glasgow was flourishing! One type of stone selected for this regeneration was porphyry, a very hard-wearing, reddish coloured, igneous rock, which was to be found and quarried at Crarae, on the shores of Loch Fyne in Argyllshire.

The supply operation was simple but very efficient. The rock was cut from the hillside, loaded onto ships in the loch and sailed up the Clyde right into the heart of Glasgow. A boat-load of the stone could be removed from the quarry in the morning and be in the city later the same afternoon.

Due to the amount of business being done, Glasgow Town Council had forged close links with the quarry, which was owned by the Duke of Argyll. To celebrate the jubilee of the Council's Statute Labour Committee, the quarry's operators, William Sim and Company, planned an historic event. Their intention was to stage the largest ever blast at the quarry by exploding a massive seven tons of gunpowder. The proposed event was advertised and an open invitation was extended to anyone who wished to attend.

And so, on the morning of Saturday 25 September 1886, over 1,300 people crowded onto Prince's Pier in Greenock, eager to board the paddle steamer, *Lord Of The Isles*, for the regular cruise to Inveraray. In order to connect with the pleasure steamer, a special excursion train, run by the Glasgow and South Western Railway Company, left

Crarae pier as it is today. Gone are the two sheds at the end of the pier.

St Enoch's Station in Glasgow at 8.30 a.m., heading direct for the departure pier. Several first-class carriages of the train had been reserved for the Councillors who were members of the Statute Labour Committee and their families. Although the rain was falling incessantly, the crowd were in high spirits. They were invited guests and as such, determined to enjoy a pleasant day's outing.

The *Lord Of The Isles* was the regular steamer on the route and a normal feature of her trips, on arrival at Crarae, was the sounding of a long blast of the ship's whistle, followed shortly thereafter by an explosion at the quarry. These prearranged displays thrilled her everyday passengers.

After having made short stops at Rothesay and Tighnabruaich on the way, the paddle steamer arrived at Crarae just after 1 p.m. The rain had eased to just a slight drizzle and with thin swirls of mist covering the tops of the hills, the vessel stood off from the pier, allowing the passengers their first view of the circular shaped quarry. The walls, over 150 feet high, appeared to be glistening, but that was due to the rain.

A number of little white cottages stood at the entrance to the quarry. There was no movement in or around them as the inhabitants had

21

been evacuated in anticipation of the enormous explosion. Nothing was being left to chance as their furniture too had been removed from the houses! The steamer then manoeuvred to the centre of the loch so that the full complement of passengers, occupying every vantage point on the vessel, was afforded an uninterrupted view of the spectacular event that was about to take place.

About 1.30 p.m. and shortly after the signal whistle had been sounded, the walls of the quarry momentarily erupted upwards, before falling back into a thick cloud of dust. The roar of the explosion was heard two or three seconds later by the passengers, by which time, a previously calculated 52,000 tons of rock had been blasted free.

Within ten minutes of the huge blast, the steamer had berthed at the pier and between 150 and 200 men, women and children were disembarking and making their way on the five minute walk along the narrow road towards the quarry entrance. Having deposited those who wished to visit the site, the *Lord Of The Isles* continued on its journey to Inveraray with the rest of its passengers.

The visitors found that the entrance to the quarry was a narrow fissure cut through the outer walls. It was about 25 yards long, but only eight or nine feet wide. With only three or four persons being able to walk abreast at any one time and the walls of the quarry towering above them, some of the visitors immediately felt claustrophobic.

Members of the Statute Labour Committee were the first to enter. As they were doing so, some of the party noticed an extremely distasteful smell, which caused them to start coughing. However, passing it off as the smell of spent gunpowder, they ignored it and continued on in. Some members of the Scottish press had also been invited to attend, as it was thought that the occasion of the huge blast would make for good publicity. The group of reporters were second to enter, just behind the main party. Mr. Faill, a Glasgow contractor with interests in the quarry, was assigned to be their guide and answer their questions.

Faill's first opinion expressed to the newspapermen was that a good deal more than the estimated 52,000 tons of rock had been displaced by the explosion. A heavy grey smoke was seen to be seeping from the fallen rocks, but no one paid any particular attention to it. After having been in the quarry for about two or three minutes, the councillor's party was confronted by a workman in an excited condition, waving his arms about and shouting for them all to

22

withdraw. Thinking that it must be because of some unexploded gunpowder, they were about to comply with the request, when one of the party, a Dr Wilson, having caught the odour of highly poisonous sulphuretted gas, shouted, 'We are in a trap. Run.'

Simultaneous with Wilson's shout, a dog in the company of one of the group barked once and fell dead. The dog's owner, a woman, bent down to pick the animal up but became unconscious and collapsed over the carcass. A young boy, who moments earlier had been playfully scrambling amongst the fallen rocks, also collapsed. Two men, going to his assistance, were also overcome by the choking fumes and fell unconcious beside him.

By now, in all parts of the quarry, more visitors were coughing, choking or collapsing. The invited guests had seen enough, and they began running back towards the entrance. This created confusion and hysteria, as they were running against the tide of people still coming through the narrow entrance, oblivious to what was happening inside. A stampede ensued, and those not affected by the poisonous gas were knocked over by others in their haste to escape. Horrible injuries were caused to people, either by falling or being pushed to the ground. Heads, faces and limbs were badly gashed on the sharp rocks.

Eventually those visitors who were able to began running down the road towards the pier. A slight breeze was blowing from the quarry in the direction of the pier, which resulted in some of them being overcome by the poisonous gas and collapsing on both sides of the road. Others, lucky enough not to be rendered unconscious, were to be found in various poses, coughing violently. A small number of passengers managed to reach the pierhead and found that the bracing sea air quickly cleared their condition. After recovering, they returned to the roadway to assist others more seriously afflicted than themselves.

Over 50 passengers had been affected by the gas. They had either become unconcious or were stricken by uncontrollable coughing fits. Some quarrymen, who seemed unaffected by the fumes, formed a search party and re-entered the quarry. They quickly located and recovered six dead bodies from within. Other victims, who had been quite seriously injured, were assisted by the quarrymen in their attempts to escape from the deadly enveloping gas. Finally the quarry was cleared of people.

Outside, the injured were lying all around. Some were motionless, while others were having convulsions, with two or three of the healthier passengers having to hold them down. The most seriously

Crarae Quarry today. Abandoned, it sits at the side of the main 'A' road.

injured were taken onto the pier, where they were tended to by some of the women in the party. Dr Wilson and a fellow colleague, a Dr Taylor, both of whom had been affected by the poisonous fumes, had recovered sufficiently to administer some medical assistance to those most in need. Eight city councillors were amongst those injured. Mr Morrison of the firm Morrison & Mason, the main contractors for the new City Chambers building, was one of the more critical victims.

The bodies of those who had perished were very quickly removed to a small shed at the end of the pier.

On the return of the *Lord Of The Isles* to the pier, the scene greeting the vessel was one of tragedy. Very quickly, passengers from the steamer went to the assistance of those ashore. A further two doctors were among those newly arrived and they gave what aid they could to their colleagues in attending to those who were suffering.

The bodies of the dead were taken on board and placed in the steamer's fore cabin along with two of the most seriously injured victims. The rest of the injured were taken to the aft cabin. As the steamer set sail for Greenock, some of the previously unaffected passengers were beginning to suffer bouts of coughing, an indication that the incapacitating fumes were still in the air, and now in the area surrounding the pier.

Just after leaving Crarae, the rain began falling heavily again and all the passengers aboard crammed into the lower decks to shelter from the elements. With the shock of the tragedy beginning to take effect, the passengers, most of whom were in wet clothing, were forced into close proximity with each other. Some of the walking injured were unable to breathe properly. This in turn led to many arguments. Numerous fights broke out as, unbelievably, some inconsiderate travellers began smoking in the crowded compartments and passages, making the situation even more intolerable.

The steamer called first at Tighnabruaich, from where telegrams were dispatched to relatives of the dead and injured. A telegram was also sent to Captain Orr, chief of the local constabulary at Greenock, asking that the vessel be met on its arrival and stating the necessity for ambulance wagons to be standing by. At one point, an opinion was voiced that the steamer should make direct for Glasgow, but it was found that the vessel only had enough coal on board to feed the boilers until Greenock.

The paddle steamer then called at Rothesay. A number of passengers disembarked at this time, unable to take any more of the nightmare trip. Eventually, the steamer reached Prince's Pier in Greenock and was met by a large crowd, who had gathered as news of the terrible tragedy had filtered through. Captain Orr and his four constables had great difficulty in keeping the waiting crowd under control, and for a number of minutes, pandemonium reigned. However, order was soon restored, and seven badly injured passengers were removed from the vessel to the summoned police ambulance wagons and taken immediately to the local infirmary.

During the night, one passed away, never having regained conciousness, bringing the total who had perished to seven.

The majority of those affected by the poisonous gas had recovered during the journey, and declined any hospital attention. Instead they preferred to catch a train from the nearby station to complete their journey to Glasgow.

As word of the tragedy spread, so newspapers picked up on the story. One brought out a special edition at 9 p.m. that night, with the sensational headline, 'Three Glasgow Magistrates Killed!'. The newsheet sold out within minutes to an eager public who were scrambling for any details of the tragedy. The truth of the matter was that two Glasgow Councillors, *not* magistrates, were amongst the dead.

Another victim, a 17-year-old youth, was the son of a Glasgow magistrate, who sadly had been on the trip and, along with his wife, was on the steamer when his son's body was brought on board.

An official enquiry into the tragedy was quickly called for and the Procurator Fiscal's office at Inveraray made the initial investigations. It was quickly established that a number of factors had contributed to the cause of the tragedy. After an explosion of gunpowder, poisonous fumes are always present. This gas, which can on occasion be a mixture of two or more gases, has a greater density than air and as a result, the fumes sink to ground level. As a consequence of the quarry being circle shaped, having high sided walls with a very narrow entrance, and the wet and 'heavy' weather, the gas could not easily disperse. An exceptionally large amount of the poisonous fumes had been released due to the huge quantities of gunpowder that had been detonated. Those entering first were not immediately affected because the fumes were low-lying. This is borne out by the fact that the dog, being much closer to the ground, was the first to perish. However, the more people entered, the greater was the disturbance of the fumes, and the victims then rapidly succumbed as the poisonous gases rose upwards.

No one was blamed for the tragic event. Some were congratulated for their actions, which saved the lives of many of the visitors, so preventing the tragedy from turning into a greater disaster.

As we admire the many red stone buildings of Glasgow, it should be remembered that some of those very stones used could have been freed from the quarry walls at Crarae on the day of the huge explosion, the day when a pleasure trip turned to tragedy.

TERROR ON THE TERRACES
The First Ibrox Stadium Collapse

The posters appeared all over Scotland advertising the forthcoming attraction. An international football match would take place on Saturday 5 April 1902 at Ibrox Park, Glasgow. It would be the 31st meeting between the 'Auld Enemies', Scotland and England.

Unlike the present day, the Scottish national team had no permanent home then, and as a result of this nomadic existence, the Scottish Football Association (SFA) convened a meeting a few weeks before the proposed match day to consider where the game would be played. It was a straight choice between either Parkhead, home of Glasgow Celtic, or Ibrox Park, home of the Rangers, as they were then known. By one vote, Ibrox was selected to be the venue.

Ibrox Park was new, having only only been in existence for about two years. As Glasgow expanded, so the need for land for housing became greater. In past years, the Rangers had had to vacate two previous grounds, at Kinning Park and at Copland Road, for that reason. The Ibrox site was their largest yet, measuring some 14 acres, and the stadium cost £20,000 to build. It was designed by the same architect who had drawn the plans for both Sheffield United and Derby County football grounds in England.

The main stand was on the south side, as it is today, while the north side was a covered terracing. The east terracing had about 50 tiers or steps, while the west terracing, with 100 steps, was twice the height. Both terracings, east and west, were uncovered and therefore, open to the elements. They were constructed in a similar manner:

27

steel columns embedded into a concrete base, with steel beams running between the columns. Wooden planking was placed over the beams and further wooden tread boards, upon which the supporters stood, were placed on top of this. To enclose everything, a fence of corrugated iron sheeting was sited at the very top of each terracing.

The playing pitch was encircled by a black cinder track, and both the pitch and the track were separated from the terracings by a wooden perimeter fence, on top of which iron railings had been specially added for the upcoming match. All told, the huge bowl of a stadium had room for 84,000 spectators.

On the day of the big match, kick-off was planned for 3.30 p.m. The forty turnstiles were opened at 12.30 p.m. and by then a fair number of spectators had already gathered, waiting to pay their shilling admission money. For the most part, these early entrants to the stadium were supporters who, having travelled great distances, had arrived early in the city.

About an hour after the opening of the gates, the slow trickle of early fans had turned into a surging mass of people. The east terracing, which was capable of accommodating 15,000, had filled to capacity first, it being the nearest to the city. Now the incoming spectators were rushing to find themselves one of the 33,000 viewing points on the vast slopes of the west terracing. Very soon this terracing began to fill up too. Some reports suggest that it was over-filled and as a consequence, just before kick-off, the huge number of supporters began a swaying motion which resulted in those at the bottom of the terracing being crushed and injured against the perimeter fence. A number of those injured persons were lifted clear and placed onto the cinder track, whilst hundreds more climbed over the fence and onto the pitch to escape injury. Chaos reigned, with newspapers being thrown by the terracing crowd to show their displeasure at those fans now milling about on both the cinder track and pitch. Mounted police were quickly on the scene and eventually managed to restore order, but such was the overcrowding, most of the displaced spectators had to take up positions elsewhere in the stadium. A large number of fans were forced to sit on the track with their backs to the fence, there being no space for them anywhere else.

While all this was going on, the two teams had arrived on the pitch, ready to begin the contest, and their appearance had a somewhat calming effect on the crowd, making the job of the police a little easier. The stairways on the west terracing became heavily congested as spectators climbed higher and higher, looking for a space, any space,

An artist's impression of the scene shortly after the west terracing collapse.
(Lang Syne Publishers, Glasgow)

somewhere in the throng of fans before the game began. At the top of the passageways, clusters of fans could be seen trying to push their way onto the terraces, as those already there were not making way for them. Eventually, the stairways became completely blocked, especially on the uppermost parts.

The match got under way, but with only a few minutes play on the clock, disaster struck on the west terracing. A portion of the highest section of the terracing gave way under the strain of the excessive number of fans, and several hundred of them were thrown to the ground about 40 feet below. As they lay there in a tangled mass of humanity, debris from the broken structure fell on top of and all around them. Some spectators, who had not fallen originally, teetered an the broken edges and tumbled into the carnage below to add to the toll. Others were pulled back from the brink by fellow supporters in the crowd.

Once again, panic rose in the west terracing crowd and the spectators at the top of the terracing surged forward to escape from the yawning gap, crushing those in front of them. For the second time that day the crowd, this time in their thousands, poured over the barricades and onto the pitch. Such was their desperation to flee from the tragedy, they tore the iron railings from their mountings in most places.

The crowd in the remainder of the stadium, unaware of the disaster and thinking that it was another unruly invasion, began shouting and gesticulating. The match was immediately halted and the players taken off the field of play. For several minutes after the collapse, only those on the west terracing were aware of the tragedy that had occurred. Eventually, the police and officials realised what had happened and very quickly went to assist. After a 15 minute break, during which rescue operations had begun, a decision was made to restart the game. Although first reports from the scene told of a number of dead and many hundreds more injured, the authorities realised that the vast majority of supporters had no knowledge of the event and to abandon the match may have led to further panic or, worse still, a riot. The six mounted police officers were called onto the pitch once more and succeeded in forcing back the fans, so that they were now standing around the touchlines.

The task of helping those trapped in the debris continued, but because of the huge number of people who had fallen, coupled with the sharp edges of broken steel and wood, the job was extremely hazardous. Police, officials and supporters worked frantically side by side in the job of rescue. The first of the injured and dead were brought out and laid on the track at the rear of the goal area. While most had suffered bruising, quite a number had sustained more serious injuries. Apart from broken arms and legs, head injuries appeared the most common and at least one man had an eye torn right out. Very quickly, this area of the track filled up. Splints were made from the rubble and many supporters offered their jackets, coats and caps. The clothing was accepted and used to secure the splints to the broken limbs. Sheets of the corrugated iron fencing from the top of the terracing were torn down and along with other larger pieces of the debris, held together with coats and jackets, were converted into

30

makeshift stretchers. These were used to convey the dead and more seriously injured across the arena to the main stand where waiting vehicles conveyed them to the city's infirmaries.

The amount of medical resources present was insufficient to cope with the enormity of the tragedy. All manner of transport was commandeered to take the injured for treatment. Cars, taxis, horse-drawn carts and even a milk float were used. The injured were taken to the Victoria, Royal and Western Infirmaries. Those being conveyed to the last mentioned hospital also had to contend with crossing the River Clyde by ferry! One sad memory of the tragedy was recalled by many of those involved, both casualties and rescuers. As the rescue work continued among the crumpled mass of bodies, the applause of the crowd, in response to some incident of the game, mingled with the moans and groans of the injured and dying, and gave the catastrophic scene an even more unnatural atmosphere.

It wasn't until the half-time break in the match, with the score at one-all, that the players and most of the spectators in the other parts of the ground discovered the extent of the disaster. Not surprisingly, some of the players did not want to go out for the second half in light of what had happened. However, they were persuaded otherwise and the match continued. Long before the end, large gaps were appearing around the stadium as fans departed for their homes, their interest in the game having all but disappeared.

The match finished at 5.30 p.m. with the score remaining one-all, and at this time, thanks to the hard work of the rescuers, only six injured persons were still awaiting transport to a hospital. Three persons had been killed outright in the tragedy, with a further 15 later succumbing to their injuries in the hospitals over the rest of the weekend.

Before the week was out, the City Fathers had met and agreed to set up a Disaster Fund for the dependants of those who had died or were severely injured. They set a target of raising at least £25,000. Whilst the Rangers were the owners of Ibrox Park, no claims for compensation could be made against them as the Scottish Football Association had leased the ground from them to stage the International. A strange outcome of this was that when the Disaster Fund was being set up, the S.F.A. stated that they were prepared to contribute £3,000, provided that they would then be relieved of all further responsibility. Two weeks later, the S.F.A. increased their offer to £5,000, but with the same condition still attached!

Two weeks after the tragedy, the number of dead had risen to 23,

31

with another 516 injured. Of that total, 125 were still hospitalised.

The Scottish Cup Final of 1902 had been planned for Ibrox Park for the Saturday following the International, but it was cancelled, as were all other organised football matches that week, as a mark of respect for those involved. When it was eventually played on 26 April at Celtic Park, it was contested by Celtic and Hibernian, the latter running out victors by a score of one-nil. Although only 16,000 fans attended the game, such was the low interest it attracted in the aftermath of such a tragic event, the entire takings were added to the Disaster Fund.

Not until 16 May, fully six weeks after the tragedy, were the final figures known regarding those involved. A total of 25 supporters died with a further 537 injured as a result of the terracing collapse. At that date, the Disaster Fund had amassed almost £16,000 and money from various events was still coming in. Donations were made by individuals, large firms and many football clubs from Scotland and England. A large number of football matches were played purely to raise the much needed cash and all 200 police officers on duty at Ibrox on that fateful day also donated their earnings to the Fund.

As is usual in the aftermath of such a terrible occurrence, an Official Inquiry was held. Yet, irrespective of what was to blame or who may have been responsible for such a tragedy, the public realised that one fact stood out above all else. Although 25 supporters died and over 500 were injured, many thousands more had a miraculous escape.

Sixty-nine years later, Ibrox was visited again by disaster when, on 2 January 1971, 66 people died in a horrendous crushing accident on Stairway 13.

FATAL ERROR
The St Enoch's Station Crash

It was late July, and the Glasgow Fair holidays were coming to an end. The passengers slowly climbed the gangplank of the steamer *Tynwald*, which sat quietly at the quayside in Douglas, Isle of Man. The departure time was scheduled for a few minutes past midnight and into the morning of Monday 27 July, 1903. Out of respect for the Sabbath, no steamers arrived at or departed the island on a Sunday.

Over 800 holidaymakers, most still dressed in their colourful holiday clothes, were aboard, and to the strains of 'Auld Lang Syne' filtering from the pierhead, the steamer set sail on its seven-hour voyage to Ardrossan in Ayrshire.

After a smooth and uneventful crossing, the steamer arrived at Ardrossan shortly before 7 a.m. The mass of human cargo disembarked from the ship and more than 300 of them boarded a train which was sitting in the nearby railway station. The train belonged to the Glasgow & South Western Railway Company and was a holiday express, specially laid on to serve the arrival of the steamers. In the preceding years, the Isle of Man had become a favourite holiday destination for many people from the West of Scotland. The railway and steamer companies had got together to provide services to complement each others' timetables and make travelling easier. Most of the passengers travelling today were heading for Glasgow, with some of them intent on going direct to their employment that morning. Their holidays would soon be a memory.

The train departed the little station at 6.58 a.m., which was eight minutes later than scheduled, and travelled through the scenic Renfrewshire countryside, stopping for the first time at Paisley. Here

33

a large number of commuters, en route to Glasgow, joined the train. By now, the twelve carriages of the express were almost full, with around 500 passengers on board.

After leaving Eglinton Street Station on Glasgow's south side, the train crossed over the Clyde by the Stockwell Street viaduct, and entered the outer limits of St Enoch's Station, the final destination, just after 8.00 a.m. By now the express was running 22 minutes late.

St Enoch's was the terminus for two railways, the Glasgow & South Western and the North British. Built in 1876 to cope with the ever-increasing amount of railway traffic from the south, the station had, until this fateful day, remained free from serious accident.

The majority of the passengers had observed the crossing over the river and realised their journey would be at an end in a few minutes. They stood up and began removing their items of luggage from the overhead racks. Being preoccupied with this, they hardly noticed that the train was travelling faster than normal in the station. It entered the tracks adjacent to Platform No.8, but instead of slowing down, careered on towards the end of the line and the station concourse.

As was the usual practice in these days, a number of passengers all along the length of the train had opened carriage doors as the train approached the platform, eager to be off quickly and avoid the crowds. At the end of the platform, the locomotive smashed into the wooden buffers, demolishing them in an instant. The noise of the impact was like an explosion and the sound was magnified as it echoed all around the enclosed station. Every passenger who was hanging from an open door was thrown down onto the hard stone platform at the moment of impact. They were lucky to receive only minor cuts and bruises. Not so fortunate were those passengers in the first two carriages behind the locomotive.

The engine appeared to be undamaged as it came to a halt after crashing through the buffers. The first carriage behind rebounded off the engine and the rear of it lifted up momentarily. At this precise moment, the second carriage, pushed from the rear by the weight and momentum of the other ten carriages and guards van, was forced under the floor level of the first carriage. The heavy iron buffers of the first carriage sliced through the wooden bodywork of the second carriage with the minimum of fuss, totally destroying four of its five compartments.

Such was the force of the collision that the rear of the first carriage was lifted high up off the rails. The top part of this carriage made contact with the station roof, which was made of glass. A large area of the roof was damaged and all the broken glass fell down on top of the first two carriages, adding to the danger. As the train finally came to rest, the carnage was all too evident. The two carriages had been forced into the space previously occupied by one, like the closing of a two-piece telescope. All that remained of the second carriage, apart from its roof which had made inroads into the preceding carriage, were fragments.

Debris was strewn over a wide area. Broken wood and glass, covered in blood, lay in great heaps on the tracks and platform.

Help was quickly on hand from fellow passengers, station porters and railway police. Almost immediately, it became apparent that the accident had resulted in a number of fatalities. Calls for assistance immediately went out to the local hospitals and a team of surgeons from Glasgow Royal Infirmary, along with ambulance wagons, attended. The medical skills were urgently required as a large number of passengers were injured, some severely.

The rescue teams began slowly to sift their way through the rubble. Quite a number of passengers were trapped by pieces of wreckage which had finished up at odd angles. Some of the them were released simply by sawing through those pieces of wood that were impeding their escape. Others who were badly injured, on occasions by whatever was ensnaring them, required gentler handling.

Temporary treatment was administered on the platform. Those who were badly injured were suffering from broken limbs and severe lacerations and were quickly conveyed in the ambulances to the nearby hospital. Those less seriously hurt were mainly affected by bruising and shock.

Stretchers were summoned and the dead were removed from the wreckage and placed gently on the platform. The injuries that had caused death had, in some cases, been severe. One body had both legs severed, whilst another had a leg and an arm torn away.

Word of the disaster spread quickly, and very soon the station was being overrun by crowds of spectators, straining to catch a glimpse of the proceedings. With trains still coming and going from other platforms, their passengers added hundreds more to the numbers of spectators within the space of one or two minutes.

It was decided to remove the bodies to a hastily prepared temporary mortuary, which had been set up in the waiting room for Platform No.1. Unfortunately, this necessitated a long journey on foot from the scene of the tragedy and through the station. As these trips

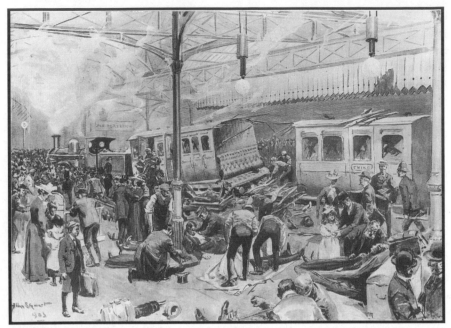

A graphic view of the tragedy on Platform No. 8. (Mary Evans Picture Library)

to the mortuary were undertaken, the crowds that had gathered surged forward in a ghoulish attempt to catch sight of the injuries of the corpses. The station police could not control the mob and eventually made the decision to clear the area of the station of all spectators. Before this could be done, the crowd of spectators gasped in shock and then immediately fell silent, when the bodies of two little children, a boy and a girl, were brought out together. More than a few of the onlookers could take no more and turned away in horror from the harrowing scene. This sight alone caused a great number of the crowd to leave the station of their own accord.

In a short space of time, the little mortuary was holding 13 bodies. The grim task of trying to identify those who had been killed then began. People from all over the city, on hearing news of the tragedy, had made their way to the station, hoping that their relatives, or friends, were not amongst those lying in the waiting room. The police formed orderly lines and began letting those persons who could provide a reasonable excuse to view the dead into the mortuary, but only six or eight at a time. All the bodies lay side by side on the floor of the small waiting room, grotesquely lit by the sun shining brightly through a window. This procession went an all day, until around 4 p.m., when the last body was identified.

The little boy and girl were identified as brother and sister, four-year-old Charles and seven-year-old Mary Wilson. But there was more horror to follow. Their father and mother were also counted among the dead. An older sister, 19-year-old Bella, had also been on the train and had escaped with a broken leg. With one stroke, an entire family had almost been wiped out.

Railway officials were quick to make statements to the press. In them, they explained that the driver of the express had said that the brakes on his locomotive had failed and by the time he had put it into reverse, the collision had occurred. Thirty-five year old Henry Northcott, and his fireman, Hamilton Kerr, who were both from Ardrossan, were said to be well acquainted with the layout of St Enoch's Station, although Northcott, not being the regular driver, was known as a 'spare driver'. Both were detained by the police shortly after the collision, pending the completion of investigations into the cause of the tragedy. Later that day, fireman Kerr was released. However, Northcott was arrested and kept in custody to await his appearance at the court the following day.

Later that Monday, two of the most seriously injured, who had been removed to the Royal Infirmary, died of their wounds. Two days later, another injured passenger also succumbed, bringing the death toll to 16. A total of 27 passengers were injured in the incident, with many others who were also hurt but refused any medical attention at the time.

Not for the first time, a Disaster Fund was set up, in the hope of providing enough cash to compensate those who had been injured, as well as the relatives of the dead. Money poured into the Fund, as the people of the city were deeply shocked, particularly at the plight of the Wilson family.

Northcott duly appeared in the Central Police Court on the morning following the tragedy. Presiding aver the appearance was Police Judge Martin. The engine driver was formally charged with culpable homicide when it was alleged that he had 'recklessly driven the train, bringing it into violent contact with the buffers, causing the carriages to collide with each other, killing a number of passengers and injuring others.' He was remanded in custody for a further 48 hours.

Two days after the tragedy, the Board of Trade opened their official Inquiry into the cause of the accident. Lieutenant Colonel Yorke, R.E., the Chief Inspecting Officer of the Railways, headed the investigation. The Inquiry was held in private in the boardroom at the headquarters of the Glasgow & South Western Railway. Yorke heard evidence from various people, mainly railway employees, including, suprisingly, Northcott himself. A station inspector gave evidence as to the rules governing any train entering the confines of a station. The main rule was that a train should travel at a speed which would allow the engine to be stopped by applying only the handbrake. This inspector had witnessed the arrival of the holiday express and estimated its speed at 20 m.p.h., which in his opinion, was excessive.

Yorke also visited the scene of the tragedy, getting a first hand look at the layout of the site. He examined both the locomotive and the carriages involved. The findings of the Inquiry were not issued at this time, probably so as not to affect Northcott's trial.

On the same day as the Inquiry opened, a number of funerals of those involved took place. None attracted a larger number of mourners than that of the Wilson family. After a service in a church in Gardner Street, Partick, the streets were lined by thousands of silent and respectful Glaswegians, as the four coffins, conveyed in two hearses, made the long journey to Lambhill Cemetery in the north of the city. All four were interred together in the same grave.

A few months later, Northcott appeared for trial before Lord Kincairney at the High Court in Glasgow. During the trial, he gave evidence on his own behalf. He stated that he was under the impression that when he entered the station, he had, as usual, been assigned a 'long dock' (platform) rather than a short one. Not until halfway down the platform did he see the mistake and by that time, it was too late to avoid the catastrophe.

Evidence was also given that due to renovation work going on in the station in the area of the platforms, the express train was scheduled to enter Platform No. 8. This not being the usual platform, Northcott was unfamiliar with it and did not know that it was between 60 and 80 yards shorter than most of the other platforms in the station!

The trial took less than a day to complete. In fact, it had lasted only six hours when a verdict was brought in. Northcott was found 'Not Guilty' of the charge and set free. From this decision, and the speed at which it was arrived at, it is safe to assume that the bad management of the Glasgow & South Western Railway Company was held to blame for the tragedy. If any doubts lingered as to their guilt, then they were dispelled in September of that year, when, at the bi-annual shareholders' meeting of the company, the investors were told that no dividend was payable to them. Instead, £11,000 was being put aside into a contingency fund, and any compensation claims arising from the tragedy would be paid from this amount.

Prior to this tragedy and thanks to its excellent safety record in comparison to other railways, the Glasgow & South Western Railway was often referred to by the sobriquet 'The Good & Safe Wee Railway'. But on that fateful day at the end of July 1903, it was none of those things.

DEATH-TRAP
The Lodging House Inferno

During the early hours of Sunday morning, 19 November 1905, Glasgow found itself in the icy grip of a fierce overnight frost. The roads and pavements had turned to a crisp white carpet and the accompanying dense freezing fog dulled nearly every sound. It was not the sort of weather one would associate with a great loss of life in a raging inferno, but it happened nonetheless.

In the east end of the city, on the corner of Watson Street and Graeme Street (now Bell Street), stood a model lodging house, unimaginatively titled 'Home No.2' to distinguish it from Home No.1 further along Watson Street. The building was three storeys high, but the attic had been converted, giving it four floors. The Home could accommodate about 360 men, each in his own small room, or cubicle as it was known. The basement was also utilised, but only as a kitchen.

The vast majority of men who used the lodging-house were unskilled labourers, who, being poorly paid, were in need of a cheap night or week's lodgings. Depending upon which floor a worker was allocated to, the cost of a bunk was 4d or 4½d per night.

Each cubicle contained a bed and a small locker for the occupant's valuables. The thin wooden walls of the rooms did not reach the ceiling, stopping between one and two feet short, so as to allow air to circulate. Strong netting covered the tops of the cubicles to prevent anyone from climbing over the walls, whether with felonious intent or not.

Although the previous night was a Saturday, the lodging-house was not filled, falling just short of capacity. About 11 p.m., when the

40

doors were locked to prevent any drunken undesirables from attempting to gain access, the first floor had 81 occupants, the second 100 and the third 105. The attic, the smallest of the four dormitories, held 63. In total, the Home held 349 residents that night.

The Home was well managed and some of its rules were more strict than other similar establishments in the city. The normal 'through the week' rule was lights out at 10.30 p.m., but it was never enforced on a Saturday night until around midnight, as, the following day being Sunday, very few of the residents were due to go to work and it was considered as a day of rest. Given this relaxation of the rule, the occupants of the lodging-house were known to enjoy a Saturday night drinking session, with large quantities of alcohol being consumed, either in the recreation room on the ground floor or in the privacy of their own cubicles.

Just after midnight, John Whalen, the house warden, carried out his final rounds of all the dormitories. During this time, he discovered a cubicle on the third floor, whose resident was reading a book by the naked light of a candle. House rules were inflexible on this matter. No candlelight or smoking was permitted in any of the rooms at any time. Whalen reprimanded the man and the candle was extinguished and consfiscated. He continued on his rounds and found that all of the inmates had retired for the night. Whalen descended the communal staircase and locked the metal security gate at the bottom before retiring to his own sleeping accommodation. For the next five or so hours, both he and the other 349 men slept soundly.

The metal gate on the staircase was there so that no resident could wander about at will through the building when all were asleep. It also served as a ticket booth where those having purchased a night's bed handed over their ticket before being allowed upstairs to their room.

Whalen awoke just after 5 a.m. that Sunday morning, and was getting himself dressed to take up his duties when he heard loud cries of 'Fire!' Running into the reception area of the ground floor, he saw a great many men, all in various states of undress, congregating on the staircase behind the locked metal gate. Shouts of 'Open the gate!' hurried him to do just that and the released men told him that a fire was raging on the third floor.

Whalen tried to make his way up the staircase to investigate matters for himself, but found his path blocked by a mass of terror-stricken men, pushing and shoving each other down the stairs. Eventually, as the surge of men thinned, he managed to fight his way upwards but

41

Home No. 2 as it looks today, with Home No. 1 in the background. Both are now derelict

he did not get very far when his way was barred again, this time by waves of impenetrable, choking smoke. As Whalen was forced back to the bottom of the staircase, he met a number of police constables entering the lodging-house who had been alerted by men on all floors smashing windows and shouting for help. The Fire Brigade, summoned by the police, also arrived on the scene at this time.

Meanwhile, inside the building, the men on the third floor who had escaped the flames were trapped. The thin but highly varnished walls of the cubicles burned quickly and fiercely and very soon most of the third floor was ablaze. The fire was assisted in no small way by the terror of some of the inmates, who had smashed windows to shout to the streets below for help. The air that got into the building through the broken windows fanned the flames.

The men discovered that they could not flee via the staircase, which was thronged with inmates and becoming enveloped with thick choking smoke. After a few moments of indecision as to what to do next, their minds were made up for them when the flames began licking at their backs. They began to fight their way *upstairs* to the attic area, hoping to find an escape route from there to the roof of the building. Some of the residents of the attic had managed to escape earlier, using the stairs, and now about 30 to 40 men were trapped there. A search of this floor revealed their only means of escape, a skylight window, with a small single pane of glass, just wide enough for a man to pass through. It stood seven feet from the floor and was securely locked. A number of the men began hammering on the glass with their bare hands but it refused to smash. A belt was produced and the buckle used as a means of trying to break it, but this effort failed too. Panic in the men rose, as by now the thick smoke was beginning to billow into the attic and the heat from the blaze below was becoming intense in the confined space of the attic. They began pushing and shoving each other in an attempt to avoid being caught up in it.

After about five minutes of confusion, Donald McNab, a crippled resident, hobbled and pushed his way through the throng of men until he was just below the skylight. Using his crutch and dealing the glass a couple of strong blows, the window broke and the cold morning air rushed in. One by one, the men climbed up and through the skylight onto the roof of the burning building. Such was their terror and their rush to escape the inferno, the fleeing men left McNab, the cripple, and another, William Nesbitt, a blind man, behind in the attic to fend for themselves. One man, John Findlay, a 35-year-old slater, on reaching the relative safety of the roof, realised what had happened and he immediately returned and dropped through the skylight back into the attic. He lifted both McNab and Nesbitt to safety through the escape hole. As he was doing this, McNab informed him that still one other inmate required saving, a man who was totally paralysed and was lying on his bed in his cubicle. After getting directions, Findlay made his way through the smoke-filled attic, going from cubicle to cubicle. Within a couple of minutes, he found the trapped man, picked him up and bodily carried him through the darkness and smoke to the broken skylight. Others on the roof, alerted by McNab, assisted in pulling the paralysed man up and onto the roof.

All of the men now on the roof were almost naked as they had no time to get dressed before looking for an escape route. Any clothes that they had managed to grab and not put on right away had been dropped in the struggle to flee. The freezing cold night air now gnawed at them and more than a few thought it ironic that they had just escaped a burning death only now to face a freezing one. The men huddled together in an effort to keep warm, but it had little effect.

Findlay, with no shirt or shoes and wearing only a pair of trousers, made sure that McNab, Nesbitt and the paraplegic were safe, sitting on the roof with their backs resting against the parapet. He then began moving about the roof, searching it as he went for some means of escape. After about half and hour, he finally found what he was looking for: a ladder. It had been left there by a chimney sweep and it connected the roof of the lodging-house with the roof of a tenement building in Graeme Street. Very slowly and one by one, the men climbed down the ladder. The men were frozen, especially their hands, and because of this, they could hardly feel anything they touched. Once on the lower roof, they found another skylight—fortunately open this time—and a police constable on hand with his lamp shining as a guide in the fog to the men. Findlay once again aided McNab, Nesbitt and the paraplegic to their final safe haven. Not content with what he had done so far, Findlay took the lamp from the constable and climbed back up the ladder and onto the roof of the blazing lodging-house. He went back and forward across the roof at least three times to ensure that no one had been left behind. No one had and he returned to safety.

During this time, members of the Fire Brigade had entered the building and begun both to fight the fire and rescue trapped and injured residents, When the blaze had been extinguished, the firemen rescued over 30 men from the building, all still alive but in an unconcious state. Some of the men recovered quickly on breathing the cold clear air, but others were in a worse condition and all forms of vehicular transport in the vicinity were commandeered to convey them up the High Street to the Royal Infirmary.

Even at that early hour on a Sunday morning, crowds of spectators had gathered as word of the calamity spread. Those fortunate enough to flee the blazing building were quickly offered coats from the crowd and blankets from the ambulances, both to keep them warm and to hide their nakedness before being taken to either the nearby police office or Home No.1.

As daylight grew and the fog slowly evaporated, the full effect of the fire could be seen. Almost all the windows on the third floor were broken and the stonework surrounds blackened by flame and smoke The remainder of the building appeared to have escaped serious damage apart from that caused by water from firemen's hoses and the stench of fumes. The bodies of the dead were removed from the ashes one by one and placed in ambulance wagons for the short journey along Graeme Street to the police office mortuary. All morning the wagons trundled back and forward along the street and there seemed no end to it.

Just before noon that Sunday, the full facts of the catastrophe were revealed. The inferno had claimed the lives of 39 men with a further 24 sufficiently injured to require hospital treatment.

It became the main topic of conversation in Glasgow that day and the crowds swelled in number until thousands were milling about Watson Street and Graeme Street. Queues formed outside the police office as anxious relatives waited for information about their loved ones.

The problem now facing the police was that of identifying the bodies. Unfortunately, those who frequented the city's model lodging-houses were normally of a type with no stable family background, many of them loners and workers from other areas of the country. Surprisingly, within three days, 35 of the dead had been positively identified and the bodies could be released to their grieving kin for family burials.

The four remaining bodies were never identified or claimed and were being buried side by side the following Friday 24 November at Sighthill Cemetery in the north of the city, when a regrettable incident occurred. One of the mourners present claimed he could identify one of the victims that was now being buried. The coffin was laid aside and the ceremony continued and the other three who had perished were laid to rest. The coffin was returned to the mortuary and the mourner provided a name and address for the deceased, but when the information was checked, the man was found to be alive and well. The body was returned to the cemetery the following day and interred next to the other three.

In the aftermath of the holocaust, the public wanted only one question answered: what had caused the fire that had claimed so many lives? The official answer was that the fire was the result of a dropped light, either from a candle or a discarded match. The most often repeated unofficial reason given was that one of inmates, waking in the small hours of that morning, lit his pipe and had a few stolen puffs from it before falling back to sleep again, leaving the pipe to smoulder away, eventually to set fire to his own cubicle and in turn the rest of the dormitory. So quickly did the fire spread, the majority of those who perished had been found still within their bunks, having been suffocated by the smoke, rather than having been burned to death.

The staff at the lodging-house gave interviews to the newspapers of the day and were at pains to point out the regulations concerning no naked lights in the rooms, yet they revealed that the finding of a badly burned pillow was an almost daily occurrence for them.

New legislation after the fire meant fire escapes had to be built. Seen here is one connecting Home No. 1 with Home No. 2

Another opinion voiced was that the majority of the inmates of the lodging-house that night were the worse for alcohol. As a result, some were so drunk that they were unable to rise from their bunks to escape, and so perished where they lay. Proof of this fact was given when, between ten and eleven o'clock that Sunday morning, a number of residents of the lodging-house appeared from the dormitories of the second floor, wiping the remains of a drunken sleep from their eyes and wanting to know what all the fuss was about!

John Findlay, the man who had rescued the three men who could do nothing for themselves, became the hero of the disaster. Once his story had been reported in all the newspapers, money from people in all walks of life began pouring in for him, from the newspaper-boy who sent in one shilling to the factory owner who sent five pounds and the offer of a job. One young lady from Fife also sent money and a proposal of marriage! Findlay became a celebrity and he even signed a contract to appear on stage for two weeks at the Britannia Theatre in Glasgow. He would be introduced to the audience, which was now a full house at every show, including the matinees, and then the three men he saved would be brought on to thank him personally. This scene brought tremendous applause each time it was played out. However, Findlay was well aware that his new found fame would not last and he was wise enough to put all the money, sent and earned, into a fund for himself, which was administered on his behalf by the Chief Constable of Glasgow. Findlay drew only enough from it each week to survive, although he later withdrew two substantial amounts from it, giving one to McNab the cripple and the other to a fund started on behalf of the other survivors. He later used the fund money to set himself up in business and quietly settled into a new life.

Home No.2 was repaired and re-opened early the following year. The number of persons it could accommodate had been cut and regulations were in the process of being enacted to ensure it, and other like buildings, provided adequate fire escapes. Glaswegians did not want to bear witness to another fiery holocaust.

DEATH IN THE SNOW
The Elliot Junction Collision

In the not too distant past, the month of December has meant danger for Scotland's railway passengers. On 10 December 1937 at Castlecary in Stirlingshire, 37 passengers lost their lives in a collision between two trains during a snowstorm. On the 28th day of the same month in 1879, a train was fighting its way across the Tay Bridge to Dundee in the middle of a hurricane when it, and the bridge, toppled into the murky river waters below with the loss of 75 lives. This latter incident has become renowned as the Tay Bridge Disaster.

On the 27th anniversary of that disaster, in 1906, and only a few miles from the Bridge, another railway catastrophe occurred that has all but faded away in the mists of time.

In the days before the nationalisation of Britain's railways, Scotland's rail travellers were well served by a number of independent operators, each covering different parts of the country. The Glasgow & South Western Railway, The Highland Railway, The North British Railway and The Caledonian Railway were four of the main ones. The latter two companies, the North British and the Caledonian, while each running their own lines, had, in 1880, pioneered a new concept of sharing railway tracks. Together they formed a new company, The Dundee & Arbroath Joint Line, to manage the 17 miles of already built double track between these two locations. It was the first joint venture of its kind in the United Kingdom. For 26 years, the tracks were in daily use, with only the odd minor mishap, until one winter's day: Friday 28 December 1906.

In the 24 hours preceding that Friday, the north-east of Scotland had been battered by a raging blizzard. The snow, constantly driven by fierce winds, had drifted and blocked the main railway line from Dundee to Aberdeen. Teams of men had set out from both Dundee and Aberdeen, and working through the night in terrible conditions, using a snow plough attached to a train, managed to clear the tracks in each direction to Arbroath. As a result, the 7.35 a.m. North British express train from Edinburgh to Aberdeen was able to leave Waverley Station on time that Friday morning, with almost a full complement of passengers aiming to make their northern destinations for the forthcoming New Year celebrations.

The express reached Arbroath on schedule, although the weather conditions were atrocious. It was snowing heavily and the wind was still gusting strongly. The train, like a number of others, could not progress any further as the line north of Arbroath had again become blocked by snow, all the way to Aberdeen.

By the middle of that afternoon, all the sidings around the station held delayed trains. The platforms, waiting rooms and local hotels were crammed with passengers caught in the storm. It gradually became obvious that any further progress north was impossible and a decision was made that trains could return to either Dundee or Edinburgh, as the lines south were still open. Passengers who had elected to abandon their trip eagerly boarded the express, impatient to begin their return journey.

An engine was called up and one of the biggest in the North British fleet was given the task of pulling the express on its return journey. The locomotive was so large that it could not fit onto the turntable at Arbroath and had to be coupled to the express carriages the way it had arrived. This meant that it would be making the return trip with the coal tender travelling first.

The blizzard still raged all around as the engine was being connected and a local Arbroath to Dundee train, run by the Caledonian company, left the station about 3.30 p.m. on its short journey south. The local train had travelled about two miles when it came to a halt at the platform of Elliot Junction Station. The driver was instructed that he would have to remain there as a goods train had been derailed about a mile further south down the line.

Meanwhile, back at Arbroath, the express was now ready to depart. Just after 3.35 p.m., the locomotive began its slow movement. The engine driver, George Gourlay, and his young fireman, Robert Irvine, both worked steadily and soon had the train travelling at almost 20 m.p.h.

The local train had now been standing stationary at Elliot Junction for almost ten minutes, waiting patiently for the signal to show

The engine of the express train on its side after the collision.

that the line ahead had been cleared. Behind it, the express train thundered along the tracks, cutting through the snowstorm. Gourlay was peering ahead, out and over the coal tender, when he saw the darkened rear of the local train loom out of the white wall of snow. He never got the chance to apply the brakes on the express, which careered into the stationary train with terrible consequences. The last two carriages of the local train were completely destroyed. Debris from the collision was strewn all over the area of the station. Most ended up at the side of the tracks, with some landing on the platform. The force of the impact was so great that some wreckage even piled up onto the overhead bridge at the scene. The wheels on the express engine, which had toppled over onto its side, were turning wildly, and steam was escaping from many punctured places in its fire-box (boiler). A young boy from one of the trains ran forward and bravely closed all the valves he could find, which shut off the escaping steam and helped reduce the amount of confusion that prevailed.

The guard on the express, a Mr Hardy, fearing that another train could arrive at any moment and add to the carnage, ran back along the track waving a red lamp and placed numerous fog signals on the line as a warning.

It was another two or three minutes before the other passengers who had escaped injury realised what had happened and they then began to help those less fortunate than themselves. By following the sounds of crying and moaning coming from below the wreckage, they were successful in locating many of those hurt. Unfortunately, on occasions, when removing the debris, the rescuers also discovered a number of passengers who had been killed outright in the collision.

Both Gourlay and Irvine had been thrown from the footplate of the locomotive at the moment of the collision. Gourlay astounded his would-be rescuers by crawling out from under his broken engine, with a badly cut ear his only injury. Irvine was not so lucky. He was found lying under the coal tender, which was completely upside down, and was pinned by it to the ground and unable to free himself.

A group of three young men, who had been passengers on the express train, were sent on foot through the snowdrifts back to Arbroath to raise the alarm and obtain any assistance they could. Some of the injured, with limbs broken and twisted, were required to be treated where they lay, even though the snow storm still seethed around them. One passenger, a nurse, tended to them and improvised by making splints from pieces of the wreckage. Those less badly injured were either carried or assisted to the station waiting room. One sad sight well remembered was of a young boy, about ten years old, who sold newspapers on the trains. All day, every day, he travelled backwards and forwards between Dundee and Arbroath, selling his latest editions. He was found thanks to his quiet but constant sobbing, trapped under a large amount of wreckage. Although both his legs were badly broken, he survived.

As darkness descended over the scene, the wind stopped blowing. The snow continued to fall heavily and, in places, it was starting to cover over the wreckage.

Upon the arrival of further helpers from Arbroath, the dead were lifted and laid on the open platform where they were covered with anything that could be found, which was a necessity, as some of the injuries that had caused their deaths were of a horrible nature.

A telegram could not be sent to Dundee requesting the assistance of a breakdown gang, as the storm had brought down the wires. However, the front end of the local train was found to have been relatively undamaged in the collision and it was quickly uncoupled from the remainder of the carriages and dispatched to Dundee, carrying the message for help.

After the initial confusion, quietness surrounded the little station. Any noise was muffled by the thick blanket of snow, and only the occasional flicker of light from a porter's lamp broke the eerie gloom. Eventually, all of the dead and injured passengers had been removed from the carnage and were taken back to Arbroath. The dead were taken to a makeshift mortuary in the local Drill Hall.

With the dead and injured removed from the platform, the recovery operation begins

Back at Elliot Junction, only the fireman Irvine remained, still trapped under the tender. All kinds of efforts were made by the rescue workers to lift the tender off him, but it was too heavy for the equipment they were using. He lay trapped for hour after hour and although covered by blankets and fed continuous hot drinks, the coldness of the night was affecting him greatly. A message was sent to distant Edinburgh for heavy lifting gear, primarily to assist in Irvine's rescue, but also to clear the tracks of the broken engine, tender and carriages. When it arrived shortly before midnight, Irvine was freed immediately and taken to Arbroath Infirmary, but during the night he died. Although the injuries he sustained in the collision were serious, it was thought that he would have survived them. His death was blamed on hypothermia as a result of having lain in the cold for more than eight hours.

Another casualty of the accident was Mr Alexander Black, who was the well-known and respected Member of Parliament for Banffshire. Despite immediate surgery on arrival at hospital, he died the following day.

By the end of the weekend, when the blizzard had blown itself out and communications were being restored with the northeast of the country, it was learned that a total of 22 passengers had been killed and a similar number injured. With the exception of Irvine, all of those who perished had been passengers on the local train.

Following usual procedures, an inquiry was ordered to be held into the circumstances surrounding the disaster, but even before it was opened, opinions were being voiced as to the cause or causes.

However, before any inquiry got under way, events took a sensational turn. On 31 December, just three days after the tragedy, Gourlay, the express train driver, was arrested at his home in Edinburgh and taken to Dundee where he was charged with the culpable homicide of those who had died in the disaster. Allegations were made that Gourlay had been intoxicated while driving the express train on the return journey.

Before his trial took place, two separate investigations were held into the cause of the disaster. The results of the Fatal Accident Inquiry were reached and published shortly after Gourlay's arrest. It blamed a number of factors for the disaster, but stopped short of naming Gourlay, so as not to affect his chances of a fair trial. A Board of Trade Inquiry was also held but its findings were not released at the time.

Gourlay's trial took place at the High Court in Edinburgh in March 1907 and lasted two days. No new evidence was forthcoming at the trial. All of it had been heard before at the two inquiries. The Court was told that trains were allowed to leave Arbroath with only short intervals of time between them, when the visibility was, at some places on the line, down to 50 yards.

The points on the line had frozen solid, again due to the adverse weather. However, this was considered insignificant when it was pointed out that southbound trains had no need to go onto another line. The signals on the line were in working order, although it was found that some may have been in the wrong position due to the weight of the snow on them causing them to droop. Even though this had occurred, the signals were still in a position indicating danger.

The most damaging evidence against Gourlay was that he had been warned by the Arbroath Stationmaster, John Grant, to proceed slowly with caution and stop at all stations on the route until he reached Dundee. It was proved that Gourlay had ignored these instructions.

A number of witnesses repeated their allegations that Gourlay was intoxicated when seen shortly after the accident, but this was explained away by one witness, a passenger on the express, who said that he had given Gourlay a large drink of brandy from his flask as treatment for the shock the engine driver was suffering from.

It took the jury only 50 minutes to decide Gourlay's fate. By a majority verdict of ten to five, they found him guilty as charged, but informed the judge that as the accused's record as a train driver was exemplary and the weather conditions exceptional, they wished the utmost leniency to be shown to him. The judge, in his speech at the end of the trial, reiterated the seriousness of the charge, but he accepted the jury's recommendations and he was going to limit the sentence on Gourlay to the lightest penalty he could impose. He then sentenced Gourlay to five months imprisonment. The sentence was later successfully appealed and much reduced, but Gourlay was by then a broken man.

The Board of Trade's Inquiry findings were published the month following the trial. All the facts were neatly gathered up and explained. Not surprisingly, Gourlay was named and held entirely responsible for the disaster.

It was an accumulation of errors, negligence and sheer bad weather that led to the deaths of 22 passengers at Elliot Junction on another black December day in the history of Scotland's railways.

A TRAGIC LAST ILLUSION
The Empire Theatre in Flames

Throughout recent history, Edinburgh, unlike the rest of Scotland, has experienced very few major disasters or tragedies. The evidence points to the city as being one of the safest in which to work and live. Unfortunately, this was not the case on Tuesday 9 May 1911, when a horrific fire almost destroyed one of the city's places of entertainment.

In the early years of this century, theatres were the most popular venues for a night out for city dwellers. At this time, one the world's greatest performers was the illusionist The Great Lafayette, as he billed himself. In 1911, at the height of his fame, Lafayette embarked on a tour of the UK, and starting on 1 May 1911, was booked to appear at Edinburgh's Empire Palace Theatre in Nicholson Street for two weeks, after which his show was to transfer to Glasgow.

As befitted an artiste of his worldwide standing, Lafayette travelled with his own troupe of about 25-strong, which included a small orchestra. As Lafayette was also the world's highest-paid entertainer, personally earning £500 per week for his current engagement, he could well afford the costs involved in maintaining this large entourage.

For the first week of the engagement, every performance displayed 'full house' notices outside and Lafayette enthralled each audience with his mystifying illusions. He was a 40-year-old American, whose real name was Sigismund Neuberger. He was unmarried, a strict disciplinarian and was considered to be something of an eccentric. His best friend was a dog called Beauty, which had been given to him by his good friend and world renowned escapologist, Harry Houdini. So

55

great was his affection for the animal that he treated it almost like a human, feeding it five-course meals at tables in the finest restaurants. The dog wore a collar of silver name tags, each of which bore a place name they had visited.

Unfortunately, on Saturday 6 May 1911, Beauty died. Lafayette was heartbroken, so much so that it was thought that he might cancel that evening's performance. All that day, attempts were being made to have the dog buried, but numerous cemeteries that were approached reacted with horror at the thought of having an animal laid to rest within their grounds. Eventually, one cemetery, Piershill in Edinburgh, agreed to Lafayette's request, but with a particular condition attached. Whenever and wherever Lafayette died, his body was to be returned to Piershill to be buried in the same grave as his pet.

With no other option open to him, Lafayette agreed to this strange contract and immediately engaged workmen to build a crypt, which would be large enough to accommodate him when the time came. What no one knew was how very close at hand that time was.

While these details were being attended to, Lafayette had his pet embalmed and placed in a crouching position in a glass case. This was then given pride of place in the suite of rooms he was occupying at the city's prestigious Caledonian Hotel, until the burial time, which was scheduled for the following Wednesday.

On the evening of Tuesday 9 May, a full house of almost 3,000 people crowded into the Empire Theatre to witness Lafayette's performance. All went well until just before 11 p.m., when the final illusion was being performed. This illusion, billed as 'The Lion's Bride', involved the appearance on the stage of a horse and a lion, both of which Lafayette owned and trained. The scene was that of a harem, and Lafayette appeared in an Eastern style costume, riding the horse. The stage was full of scantily dressed women, acting the parts of residents of the harem. Soon, a young girl was dragged into view screaming, and when she refused the advances of Lafayette, the cage containing the lion was revealed to the audience. To the gasps and squeals of the audience, the young girl was thrown into the cage with the lion, which immediately leapt towards her. The girl was in no real danger as the beast was kept from approaching her by means of a trap door, although to the audience's view, the lion still appeared to be in the cage. This part of the illusion was thought to have been accomplished by the use of unseen mirrors. By deception and deft movement, Lafayette himself had entered the cage, dressed in a lion's costume. He had first of all exchanged places with a double on stage, probably during the squealing of the audience, when all eyes were on the girl and the lion, donned the beast's outfit and by means of a trap door, exchanged places with the real lion and entered the cage. This was the illusion. All was revealed when Lafayette removed the lion's head and fired off a volley of blank pistol shots at both the real lion and his stand-in double, at which point the illusion ended. On this particular night, the illusion was performed right up until the moment Lafayette pulled the head from the costume to reveal himself.

Meanwhile, unknown to the actors, an electric wire had fused just above where they stood in the centre of the stage. A sheet of flame then travelled up the bare wire to a large canvas painting hanging over the stage, which caught fire immediately. Some of the staff, working high above the stage in the flies, tried to put the fire out, but failed. A number of lanterns, suspended over the set, began to burn fiercely and the first the actors or audience knew about the problems was when one fell onto the stage and exploded, setting fire to the flimsy furnishings.

The performance was stopped when the theatre's fire safety curtain was lowered. Unfortunately, some of the set decorations, scattered by the fleeing actors, stopped the curtain from making contact with the floor. A gap of just over a foot caused enough draught to fan the flames behind the curtain, and within seconds the area was well ablaze.

The audience still sat in their seats, in silence, unsure as to whether or not this had all been part of the act. Not one of them moved until the manager of the theatre, Mr C B Fontaine, appeared on stage in front of the safety curtain. He had the presence of mind to instruct the orchestra to play 'God Save the King'. As the audience rose en masse, they could clearly see bright fingers of flame streaking out from the gap under the safety curtain and across the heads of those in the orchestra pit. The audience needed no second warning. With the assistance of the theatre staff, the premises were cleared in about three minutes. There was some panic, but of a nature that caused only minor injuries. At certain points of exit, there were the expected crushes but these resulted in nothing more than a twisted arm or sprained ankle.

Once outside, the audience gathered in the street to watch the proceedings. There they witnessed the strange sight of some of the performers milling around in the crowds, still dressed in their brightly coloured stage costumes.

A few streets away, in Forrest Road, at the local Territorial Army Barracks, the officers and men saw the red glow in the darkness and

The Great Lafayette, dressed in Sultan's costume, in the programme for his ill-fated show. (The Scotsman Publications)

quickly realised that something awful was taking place. Over 200 soldiers, in full uniform, made their way to the scene. They found there
was already a police presence and the Fire Brigade were just arriving.
In an effort to restore order, the Territorial Army adopted the role of
crowd stewards, guiding the people away from the scene, allowing
room for the firemen to run out their hoses. However, some members of the crowd, described in reports of the time as 'rough elements', failed to respond to the requests to move away and the soldiers resorted to linking rifles to force these sections of spectators to
one side. The rowdies didn't take too kindly to this treatment and
sporadic fighting broke out. They were no match for the soldiers and
the disturbances were quelled very quickly. The worst offenders were
arrested and led away by police.

The ferocity of the blaze was such that the firemen could not enter
the building. Instead, they trained their hoses on it from any vantage
point they could find, concentrating on the stage area. The theatre
was situated in an area of tenement dwelling houses and a large number
of residents were evacuated when fears rose that the flames would
spread to adjoining buildings.

Meanwhile, inside the theatre, the stage area had quickly turned
into a raging inferno. The draught coming through the gap at the
bottom of the safety curtain was fanning the flames and the spread of
the fire was accelerated even more as the exit doors had been left
open in the wake of the fleeing audience, allowing a breeze of night
air into the auditorium. For the performers, escape from the stage
area was made all the more difficult as Lafayette had insisted that all
doors leading to and from it were locked when he was performing.
His reasons for these instructions were to ensure that the secrets of
his illusions could not be seen by anyone outside his company and
more importantly that the lion, if it got loose, could not escape. Those
actors who had escaped from the stage made towards the rear of the
theatre where their dressing rooms were situated, only to find the
narrow corridors filled with dense, choking smoke.

About 30 minutes after the start of the fire, the huge iron safety
curtain fell backwards onto the stage, and its tremendous weight
crushed the lion's cage as if it were a matchbox.

One man, Edward Bussell, who was employed by Lafayette as a
scenic artist, had been above the stage when the blaze broke out. He
quickly rescued what he at first thought were two children. They were
in fact, two midget actors, employed to play child parts in various
illusions. Bussell led them to what he later decribed as a 'place of

safety', leaving them there to return to the stage area to see if he could assist anyone else. Just after he left them, Thomas Baines, an actor in Layfayette's troupe, was making his escape when he came upon the two sitting in a corridor which was quickly filling up with smoke. He picked up both, one under each arm, and moved quickly away.

Outside, thousands more spectators had arrived on the scene, alerted by the blaze which had lit up Edinburgh's night sky. Flames were leaping from the roof of the theatre and sparks were being hurled onto nearby buildings and into the streets.

Eventually, the roof above the stage fell in, exposing the auditorium to the thousands of spectators. It was relatively undamaged by the fire but was eerily lit up by the flames still raging.

As the firemen gained the upper hand and brought the blaze under control, a party of them entered the building, hoping to rescue anyone who might, by some miracle, be still alive. On first entering, the search party had to avoid the stage area, as the massive iron safety curtain almost completely covered it and was still too hot to touch. Even if they could have laid hands on it, it is unlikely they would have been able to lift it, such was its weight. Instead, they confined the search to the dressing rooms area. Very quickly, two dead bodies were recovered on a landing, lying side by side with their heads resting on the stairs. A few feet away lay an exit door which would have led to the outside and safety. In one dressing room, the firemen found another three corpses. These were the bodies of the two midget actors. The other body was that of Baines, the man who had picked them up in his arms.

The search continued slowly, hour after hour. By now, the iron safety curtain had cooled, thanks to the water played on it by the firemen still outside. This allowed a number of the search party to crawl below it and into the area under the stage. In this section was a passageway that led directly to Lafayette's dressing room. As they made their way along the corridor, the men made an unbelievable discovery when they found a member of the cast who was still breathing. He was quickly removed from the theatre and rushed to the Western Infirmary, but despite the medical attention, he failed to respond and died. Another body, which was later identified as one of Lafayette's bandsmen, was also recovered in this corridor.

James Neilson, a stage-hand who lived locally, was working in the flies of the theatre and managed to escape via a window in the roof into a yard next to the hall. He was found in a bad way and removed to hospital, where he later died of his severe burns.

Finally, the search party reached Lafayette's dressing room, only to find that the door had already been smashed in. There was no sign of Lafayette within the room.

Just after 4 a.m. a roll call was taken which confirmed that eight people were dead and a further two unaccounted for. One of those missing was Lafayette. When word of this fact got around to the spectators, more than a few made the same comment. Had Lafayette performed some special magic and vanished completely?

Once more, the search party entered the building. There were no flames, only billows of smoke slowly rising from the still smouldering debris. Within a short space of time, just after 5 a.m. the firemen came upon two dead animals, the horse and the lion. Nearby, they found a dead body, which was dressed in the remnants of a Sultan's outfit. It was identified as The Great Lafayette. The body, horribly burned and disfigured, was taken to the city mortuary. Arrangements were made to convey it to Glasgow by train for cremation, which had been the wish of Lafayette himself. At this time, Edinburgh had no cremation facilities of its own.

Lafayette's London manager, a Mr Nisbet, arrived in the city early on Wednesday afternoon. After listening to what had happened, Nisbet felt uneasy and voiced his concerns to Firemaster Pordage, the officer-in-charge. The basis of Nisbet's anxiety was that Lafayette's valuable rings, which he wore on both hands, were missing. One ring alone was valued at over £500. These details were corroborated by Lafayette's business manager, a Mr Collins, who had also arrived in the city.

Back at the theatre, the search was continuing for the last remaining person not accounted for, Charles Richards, a musician in Lafayette's company. The firemen were also told to keep a lookout for the missing jewellery. All day the search continued, mainly in the area under the stage, until about 5.30 p.m. that night, when one of the firemen found a sword. It was identified as one worn by Lafayette, although it was hard to recognise as such as it had been completely distorted by the intense heat. Within minutes, the same fireman found another body. As it was being removed, Nisbet and Collins arrived on the scene and positively identified it as being Lafayette. As the corpse was burned totally beyond recognition, the identification was based on the rings found lying under the body. There was no doubt this time: the great illusionist had been found.

It is thought that Lafayette perished very soon after the blaze began. He had fallen through one of the trap doors in the floor of the

The grave of both Lafayette and his dog Beauty. A headstone was erected later

stage during the confusion, injuring himself so badly that he could not even crawl away before the flames engulfed him. This of course meant that the authorities had cremated the wrong body. The ashes of the body in the Sultan's costume had already been returned from Glasgow to the mortuary and they now realised that these were the last remains of Charles Richards.

The simple explanation given for the confusion was that during the enactment of the last illusion, and unknown to the authorities, Richards acted as a double for Lafayette. This allowed the illusionist to appear in the lion's cage. Due to the lateness of the hour, Lafayette's body was placed in a coffin and put in his own Mercedes motor car. The vehicle then sped through the night from Edinburgh to Glasgow, arriving at the Western Necropolis (Maryhill Crematorium) just after midnight. It was out of hours for any cremation, but special disposition had been sought and granted.

The coffin was opened, and once officials were satisfied that it really was the body of Lafayette this time, the required forms were completed and the service proceeded.

In the meantime, Lafayette's dog Beauty had been laid to rest in accordance with his wishes. In the illusionist's absence, the ceremony was overseen by both his managers.

On Sunday 14 May 1911, the funeral of The Great Lafayette himself took place. The cortege, 20 carriages long, slowly passed the Caledonian Hotel, and along Princes Street. Thousands of people stood three or four deep, as they lined the route in silence.

Once at Piershill cemetery, the vault Lafayette had ordered to be built only a few days before lay open to receive him. Lafayette's ashes were contained in an oak casket, which was also lead lined and hermetically sealed. The casket was placed between the open front paws of Beauty and the glass case was replaced in the vault. Some mourners thought that this act had overtones of a pagan ritual but said nothing at the time. A heavy slab then covered the grave, bearing an inscription mainly relating to the dog. A hasty addition in the bottom right corner showed only the words, 'The Great Lafayette'. A headstone was erected later that same year.

All told, ten people died in the raging inferno at the Empire Theatre. Three of them were local men, all employed as stage-hands, while the other seven were members of the touring show. The loss of life could have been much greater had it not been for the fire safety curtain, which confined the blaze to the stage area, and the calm evacuation of the audience.

The Empire Theatre was later re-built and still stands today. After many years as a bingo hall it was restored to its former splendour and now functions as the prestigious Festival Theatre.

Lafayette left over £120,000 in his will, which his only relative, a brother, inherited. However, the secrets of Lafayette's many illusions did not change hands, as all his papers were consumed in the fire. In life, Lafayette had many secrets, and in death, he took most them with him.

ENTOMBED
The Last Dive of Submarine K.13

Mention the word submarine and it conjures up images of a black sleek-hulled vessel, capable of travelling above or below the surfaces of the world's oceans. Silent, sometimes unseen, a powerful emissary of death, or peace, depending on your viewpoint. The images are modern ones.

In 1917, at the height of the hostilities in World War I, submarines were a relatively new concept. Only the year before, the first steam submarine in the Royal Navy, HMS *Swordfish*, had been built by Scotts of Greenock. At this time, Fairfields Shipbuilders, of Govan, like every other shipyard, were heavily engaged in building all manner of vessels needed for the war effort: warships, destroyers, cruisers and the new improved-design submarine.

The yard had already built four submarines during 1916, all of them E-class, namely E.37, E.38, E.47 and E.48, and towards the latter half of that year, received Admiralty plans for the new K-class submarine. These were bigger, faster and more modern than the previous design, but not necessarily better. Fairfields had been commissioned to build two of the new K-class submarines (K.13 and K.14), whilst Scotts and Beardmores had orders for one apiece (K.15 and K.16 respectively).

The design of these submarines was far from sleek. The method of propulsion was steam, which meant oil-fired furnaces. This necessitated the presence of two funnels on the after deck of the submarine. Added to that, four air intakes, through which air was fed into the furnaces, were also situated in this area of the vessel. Prior to submerging, the funnels were retracted and made watertight by the closing

64

of hatches. The air intakes were secured by covers known as mush-rooms, so called because of their shape. The furnaces were extin-guished using water, which caused tremendous amounts of steam to build up in the boiler room. All told, there were between 25 and 30 openings or vents in the submarine, which had to be made watertight before any submerging could occur. Once under the surface, the sub-marine used electric motors for power.

The first submarine, given Fairfields yard number 522, was launched on 11 November 1916 and named K.13. She was, on this date, at 340 feet in length and 1,800 tons, the largest submarine in the world. After fitting out, K.13 began her sea trials on 19 January 1917 and successfully completed her first diving trial the following day.

As was (and still is) normal procedure with Admiralty contracts, all vessels commissioned by them were required to pass acceptance trials prior to being handed over officially for service in the Royal Navy. The Admiralty trials took place on 29 January 1917 in the relatively quiet winter waters of the Gareloch on the Clyde. With a complement of 79 men, which included Naval officers and ratings and Fairfield employees, the trials lasted for about two hours, with K.13 being submerged at a depth of about 80 feet for almost all of this period, without incident. The Admiralty experts on board checked and tested all the equipment, except the boiler room ventilators and the funnel covers. This was due to the excessive heat within the boiler room.

When K.13 surfaced at the completion of the trials, she was ac-cepted by the Admiralty and duly handed over. Under normal cir-cumstances this would have meant the vessel returning to the ship-yard to await the assigning of a crew. On this occasion, the Admiralty men decided on one more dive, of a short duration, to check the aforementioned funnel covers and boiler room ventilators.

K.13 slipped below the surface of the Gareloch and disaster im-mediately struck the vessel. She had dived with the mushroom hatches fully opened, causing the after section of the submarine to become flooded. The vessel very quickly sank, coming to rest on the bottom of the loch, 38 feet below, trapping 48 men in the forward area. The 31 men who had been in the aft section had perished almost instantaneously.

Unknown to those on board K.13, the commander of submarine E50, which was nearby, had seen the final dive of the now stricken vessel. He did not like the way she had submerged, probably as he

K.13 after her Gareloch sinking and showing her K.22 markings. Note boiler hatches at extreme right.

had seen the open hatches or the water disturbance as it flooded in through the air intakes. He quickly marked the spot then raised the alarm. Rescue operations were begun without delay.

After being trapped for several hours, the prospects for the surviving 48 men in the forward area looked bleak. Not all of the men were navy personnel. There were a number of civilians, including the manager of Fairfields submarine department, a Mr McLean. He had immediately taken charge of the air compressors and containers, and using his skill and knowledge, did much to provide an air supply to keep the entombed men alive. However, time was of the essence as the air supply would not last indefinitely.

Meanwhile, on the surface, the rescuers were encountering problems. They were dealing with something new. Never before had they tried to rescue men from a sunken submarine. They were also unaware that one half of the submarine had been flooded, although it is possible they may have surmised this from the eyewitness account of the commander of E.50. Still, they were on the surface and oblivious to what was happening within K.13.

One of the Naval officers on board the sunken submarine, Commander Francis Goodhart, DSO, who had been earmarked to become Captain of the soon-to-be-built K.14, had been acting as an observer of the trials. He realised the need to get a message of some sort to the rescuers, and consulted with K.13's commanding officer to put forward his idea for an escape attempt, and at the same time, volunteered to be the person to make that attempt. The commanding officer, Commander Godfrey Herbert, DSO, agreed to the plan. Together, both men went to the area leading up into the conning tower, Herbert being there only to assist Goodhart in his attempt. Before going any further, Goodhart produced a small tin cylinder, into which he placed written instructions to the rescuers above. After sealing the tin, he secured it in his belt. Turning to Herbert he said, by way of explanation, 'If I don't get up, the tin cylinder will.' As they stood on the ladder leading up and into the conning tower hatch, the area was flooded with water up to their waists. The high pressure air was turned on, filling the space between water and tower lid. The clips of the lid were knocked off and the hatch opened. The air pressure from within kept out the ice-cold loch waters. Goodhart then stood up, took a last deep breath and pushed himself upwards. Tragically, the high pressure air from inside the conning tower forced Goodhart against the superstructure of the submarine and he was killed instantly. Herbert, in trying to assist his colleague, was, by the same air pressure, forced up through the tower and reached the surface unharmed. Herbert no doubt surprised his would be rescuers on the surface by his sudden appearance from the depths. He was able to inform them of all the problems affecting K.13 and a plan was very quickly drawn up for the rescue of the remaining survivors.

Salvage experts were summoned and divers went down to the submarine and attached armoured air pipes to the air intakes on the hull, allowing the 46 men still trapped to breathe more easily. Working day and night, the salvage team placed steel hawsers and cables under the forward section of K.13 and by this method, managed to raise this end of the submarine above the surface of the loch. The rescuers then got to work on burning a hole in the exposed hull, large enough for those trapped to escape through. At one point, one of the rescuers using an acetylene torch to burn the proposed escape hole found that the flame had been blown out by a gust of wind. After calling for a box of matches to re-light the torch, he was amazed to see the outstretched arm of one of the trapped men appearing from out of the submarine, with the hand holding a box of the much needed matches! There are no records to say whether this gesture was accompanied by any remarks. However, this incident helps in understanding the mentality of the men, all volunteers, who served aboard the submarine fleet. They were better paid than those sailors serving in other branches of the Royal Navy, the difference in pay being commonly known as 'danger money'. Even at that, there was no shortage of volunteers.

The rescuers finally burned a hole in K.13's hull, and 57 hours after she sank, 46 men, 13 of them Fairfield employees, scrambled to safety.

It took several more weeks of round-the-clock salvage work before the rescuers could lift K.13 off the bottom of the Gareloch and to the surface. They were mystified to find that the aft section of the vessel contained only 29 bodies. Those of Engineer Lieutenant Lane and John Steel, foreman of Fairfield's engine department, were missing! The mystery was very quickly solved when a female employee of a Shandon hotel, which overlooked the Gareloch, notified the authorities that shortly after seeing K.13 submerge for the final time, she had observed two bodies floating in the water at the scene. She had told the same story at the time of the tragedy, but it had been dismissed as nonsense. The strong currents in the loch had swept both bodies away before any rescuers had arrived at the scene. Lane's body was found almost two months later, washed up on a beach further down the Clyde estuary. Special permission was obtained and the communal grave in the small cemetery at Faslane, overlooking the Gareloch, that was the final resting place for those who perished in K.13, was opened and Lane's body was laid beside his colleagues. Steel's body was never recovered.

A total of 26 Naval personnel and six Fairfield workers died in the tragedy. His Majesty, King George V, sent a personal message of sympathy to all the relatives. The workforce of the shipyard held a collection, to which the management contributed the sum of £100, and a memorial in the shape of a granite drinking fountain was erected in Elder Park, Govan, opposite the main offices of Fairfield Shipbuilders. The memorial remains there to this day. The names of those who perished are inscribed on the sides. A plaque was later added at the foot of the memorial, dedicated to those who served aboard submarines during World War II.

On 19 February an Admiralty Board of Inquiry was convened in the boardroom of Fairfield's Yard. After hearing all the available evidence, the Inquiry laid the blame for the tragedy squarely on the shoulders of Engineer-Lieutenant Lane, who, in his capacity as Officer-in-Charge of the boiler room, failed to ensure that the mushroom covers were closed before proceeding to dive.

As the Board of Inquiry was held in the time between the rescue of the trapped men and the final lifting of the submarine, their decision to discontinue the practice of allocating the number 13 to submarines meant that the vessel's name would be changed. She sank as K.13 and was raised as K.22. Never before, or since, has a vessel had its name changed whilst still sunk. The decision had been made but no official explanation was forthcoming. Perhaps the truth of the matter lay in the universal superstition surrounding the number 13!

As it was a time of war, severe newspaper reporting restrictions were in force and no information was published concerning the tragedy.

The memorial fountain in Elder park, Glasgow, opposite Fairfield's Shipyard

Only those involved at the shipyard and in the subsequent salvage operation and members of the public, who had learned by word of mouth, knew what had befallen HM Submarine K.13.

In April 1918, a newspaper announcement was made to the effect:

'The King has approved the posthumous award of the Albert Medal in Gold for gallantry in saving life at sea to Commander Francis H H Goodheart, DSO, RN.' Today, the equivalent award would be the George Cross. The citation went on briefly to describe Goodhart's bravery, without mentioning specific details such as date, location, vessel or numbers involved. Reporting restrictions were still in place. Indeed, this was the first time any newspaper had carried an article on the tragedy.

Commander Herbert was promoted to Captain and survived the War. Mr McLean continued working with Fairfields in the submarine department and was probably involved later in 1917 when the yard launched submarine K.14, an exact replica of the tragic K.13. Fairfields continued to build submarines until the end of the war the following year.

The last words on the tragedy should be left to Lord Fisher, First Sea Lord, when he said, 'The most fatal error imaginable would be to put steam engines in a submarine.' He was speaking to Vice-Admiral Sir John Jellicoe on 1 June 1913, almost four years before K.13 met her end! K.13 was re-fitted and put into service.

Almost a year to the day later, as K.22, she was to play a leading part in another sea tragedy of the Great War featuring K-class submarines, in an incident in the Forth Estuary that became known as the Battle of May Island. On 31 January, 1918, a Royal Navy flotilla of battleships, destroyers, cruisers and submarines sailed down the Firth of Forth in single file in the dead of night. For reasons too numerous to go into here, one submarine (K.22, alias K.13) rammed and sank another submarine and in the confusion of the ensuing rescue operations, another submarine was sunk, this time after colliding with a destroyer, and those men in the water were run down and churned up by their own ships. That night, just off May Island, 103 men died with the enemy nowhere in sight.

K.22 was scrapped in 1926, never having fired a shot in anger.

'THE BRAVE THAT ARE NO MORE'
The Stornoway Shipwreck

When the last shot of World War I was fired in November 1918, the residents of the Isle of Lewis in the Outer Hebrides celebrated as much as any other group of people. Not for one minute did they expect that seven weeks after their rejoicing, their peaceful corner of Scotland would bear witness to a most atrocious disaster, one that was to affect the entire island.

On New Year's Eve, 1918, more than 500 Army and Navy men, returning from the War, reached the railhead at Kyle of Lochalsh on the Scottish mainland. The men were heading home to Lewis, some of them for the first time since joining up at the start of the War, to enjoy some well-earned New Year's leave. The regular MacBrayne's Western Isles mail steamer *Sheila* could not cope with the large numbers of servicemen, and the authorities, anxious to have the men home in time for the celebrations, ordered HMS *Iolaire*, the parent ship of the Stornoway Naval Base, to attend at Kyle and uplift the remaining men. When word of this reached the quayside, the army personnel and civilians were allocated travel on the regular ferry, while the naval ratings eagerly awaited the arrival of the *Iolaire*.

Some of the men remembered the vessel as sleek, reliable and fast, as she had originally been a luxury steam-powered yacht, which was often seen in Scottish waters and which had been pressed into service as a submarine hunter to help the war effort. Unbeknown to them, the *Iolaire* had been replaced about six weeks earlier with an older and smaller ship, named *Amaltheae*. The *Amaltheae* had been hired by the Government in 1915 and, on her posting to Stornoway, was given the name *Iolaire,* while the departing *Iolaire* was renamed *Amaltheae.* This was the Admiralty's idea of easy and convenient administration! When the *Iolaire* arrived at Kyle, an incident occurred which with hindsight could have been considered an omen of what was to happen later. The vessel collided heavily with the pier. The ship sustained some damage, but after a quick inspection, it was decided that this was superficial and the men began boarding the ship. At 8 p.m. she departed the dock carrying over 250 ratings and 23 crew members.

Ahead lay a six-hour voyage over an expanse of water called the Minch, which is notorious for its rough conditions. However, on this particular night, the weather was reasonably good. With a clear sky and a slight breeze, the swell of the open sea was moderate. Nonetheless it was bitterly cold and, in an effort to keep warm, some of the men found spaces inside the vessel in the saloons, but most remained outside on the open decks.

Once out of the shelter of Skye and into the open sea, the wind picked up, almost to gale force, and began churning up the waters of the Minch. It did not dampen the spirits of those on board, who were singing songs in their native Gaelic to pass the time on the journey.

Just before 2 a.m. on New Year's Day 1919, the *Iolaire* was approaching Stornoway Harbour. Some of those aboard, seeing the lighthouse at Arnish and realising they would be alongside the pier in a few minutes, began to collect their kit bags. Inexplicably, the *Iolaire* continued on past the harbour entrance and seemed set on a course to run aground at a place called Holm Point. That it did not do so was no consolation. The *Iolaire* came to an abrupt stop with a mixture of loud scraping and crunching sounds, followed immediately by a severe roll onto her starboard side. The force of the impact caused men to fall over and many were injured. In the pitch darkness, confusion reigned. After a few minutes, it became clear that the *Iolaire* had struck a group of jagged rocks, known locally as the 'Beasts of Holm', which lay 50 yards from the shore and about 300 yards beyond the harbour entrance.

Even as they assessed their predicament, with the ship listing so heavily, the sea was breaking over the decks and some of the men were washed overboard and drowned. Over 60 men, seeing the safety of the shore so very close to them, immediately jumped into the sea, which was a boiling cauldron of foam, spray and huge waves. The wind, accompanied by sleet and snow, was howling. The men in the

A lifeboat from the Iolaire *washed up on the beach at Holm Point*
(Daily Record)

water were trapped between the ship and the rocks. A combination of both wind and sea forced the stricken vessel on top of the men in the water, pushing them under the surface. Within minutes, all the men had drowned. Not one had made the shoreline.

Other men, seeing what had happened to their comrades who had jumped overboard, ran to the port side, which at this time was away from the rocks, and immediately set about launching the only two lifeboats there. About 40 of the men crammed into the small boats, but as soon as they reached the water, both were swamped by waves, crushed against the side of the *Iolaire* and sank. Only one man was thought to have scrambled back on board to the relative safety of the larger vessel. The *Iolaire*'s whistle was being sounded continually and two or three distress rockets were fired into the darkness. By their light, those left on board could see the full extent of their predicament. There seemed to be no avenue of escape from the stranded vessel and it did not take very long before panic began to rise.

The high seas and strong winds were relentlessly pounding the *Iolaire* and her position on the rocks was changing constantly. One minute she was starboard side to the shore, the next she was stern on.

73

At one point, when the ship's stern came around and was nearest to shore, almost 100 men ran aft and dropped from this part of the vessel into the sea. Yet again the *Iolaire* was buffeted by the elements and her stern came round once more and this time landed on top of the men now in the water. The propellers cut into some of them, whilst others were forced against the rocks by the wash of the rotors. The end result was the same. Not one survived.

Those still on board had witnessed the carnage that had befallen their comrades in the sea and considered that abandoning ship was no longer an option. They elected to stay aboard the stricken vessel for the very small amount of protection it offered. The *Iolaire* then turned broadside onto the shore, and only a very few men attempted to get into what were relatively calm waters between the vessel and the rocks, thanks to the temporary shelter from the wind provided by the ship. One of those men had, by means of a rope hanging from one of the decks, eased himself from the ship into the sea and then attempted to swim towards the rocks. He found himself entangled in numerous ropes which had been discarded and which almost dragged him under the surface to his death. Somehow, he managed to free himself, but as he neared the rocks, he realised that the swell of the enraged sea was too great and he was sure that he would be driven onto the reef and killed. Just at this moment, a huge wave swept him up and over the rocks and onto the shore. He had been in the water for over half an hour.

Bravely, he immediately tried to assist those still on board by clambering back onto the cluster of rocks in an effort to get a line to the vessel. Twice he was swept from the rocks by the huge seas, but he was fortunate to regain his place on the ledge each time. As he scrambled back onto the rocks for the second time, totally exhausted, he saw that another man had reached the shore and was carrying a line from the vessel. The line was pulled ashore and attached to it was a thicker hawser. Once secured, those on board began using this line to make their escape from the stricken vessel. One by one, the servicemen pulled themselves, hand over hand, along the line. They only needed to use the rope until they reached just beyond the rocks, where they could fall into calm waters next to the shore and walk up the beach.

Still the *Iolaire* was moving uncontrollably, which caused the line to go slack and taut alternately. When slack, the men holding onto the line were pitched into the water and when the vessel moved again, tightening the hawser with a snap, some of them were catapulted into the sea and subsequently drowned. Apart from a very few who had managed to swim ashore, all of the men saved were thanks to this rope. After it had been in place for about only 10 or 15 minutes, the *Iolaire* dropped away from the shore and the line snapped with a loud crack. There had only been enough time for about 60 men to save themselves.

The *Iolaire* was being lifted by the heavy seas and tossed onto the jagged rocks with sickening thuds. Eventually, she was forced completely over the reef and now lay between the rocks and the shoreline. She had been taking in water since the first impact on the reef, and was now, about an hour and a half later, almost completely flooded. Within minutes, she turned over and sank to the bottom. As she was going under, a tremendous explosion rocked her when the boilers blew up. Her masts, one of which was unbroken, still showed above the surface, marking her position.

Unbelievably, one man was clinging to the unbroken mast. He had ended up there when he could find no other means of escape and had been joined by two others. Sadly, these latter two men could not hang on due to the extreme cold and had fallen away into the sea and drowned.

The alarm had been raised in Stornoway about the terrible tragedy that was unfolding and the harbour life-saving equipment was dispatched to the scene. Although the *Iolaire* was only 300 yards from the harbour, the apparatus had to travel more than a mile by road to get to the site. Normally pulled by two horses, which for some unknown reason were not available this night, the equipment had to be manhandled by 19 men. It took quite a time to get it to the scene as it weighed more than a ton. By the time it did arrive, it was of no use. The *Iolaire* had sunk.

By dawn, as word spread throughout the island, large crowds gathered on the shore, but they were not idle spectators. Almost everyone was looking for news of their relatives or of their friends. So great was the loss of life that almost no community on the island was untouched by the tragedy. Bodies were lying scattered all over the beach, just where the stormy waters had tossed them ashore. Even more corpses were to be found floating in the now-still waters of the cove.

A number of small boats were launched and began to search in the area around the sunken *Iolaire* with grappling hooks in an attempt to recover more of the dead. One boat managed to effect the rescue of the man still clinging to the mast. He was exhausted, but soon recovered. A gruesome sight, repeated many times, was the recovery of corpses which had sustained terrible injuries. These wounds were caused by the victims being dashed against the jagged rocks.

As each grey hour passed, more and more bodies were reclaimed from their watery graves and placed, row upon row, on a nearby grass embankment to await identification. All morning, brightly coloured carts full of relatives arrived. Their loved ones were identified and removed from the scene in coffins on the back of the carts.

A disaster centre was set up in Stornoway and all those survivors who were able to report there were instructed to do so as soon as possible. The reasons were twofold. The survivors were to be interviewed so that an idea of how the tragedy occurred could be formed. Secondly, as there was no passenger list, it was in effect a 'roll-call' to find out how many had been aboard the *Iolaire* the previous night. For one survivor, the *Iolaire* disaster had been his *third* shipwreck. His previous two experiences had been during the War, when both vessels in which he was serving had been torpedoed and sunk! By noon on New Year's Day, seventy servicemen and five crew members had reported, or had someone report for them, to the disaster headquarters. All told, 186 servicemen and 19 crew members had perished in the worst ever disaster witnessed in the Outer Hebrides. The apportioning of blame for the disaster was swift. Allegations that the crew, and more especially, the master of the vessel were drunk were the most repeated. The collision with the pier at Kyle was cited as additional evidence of this charge. Unfortunately, as all of the officers and the majority of the crew had perished in the tragedy, there was no-one able to refute these rumours at the time and they gained considerable currency.

For the whole of the week following the disaster, funerals took place each day in every corner of the island. What should have been a time of celebration of the return of loved ones, and of a New Year free from the monstrosity of war, held no joy for the islanders.

As is usual in any case of this magnitude, a Court of Inquiry was set up and, on this occasion was held in public, as the people of Lewis had a right to know what had happened to their loved ones. Principal Sheriff MacIntosh presided over a jury of seven. Thirty witnesses were called to give evidence, but nothing that had not been published in the newspapers came to light. The jury retired after hearing all the evidence and returned an hour later with the following conclusions and recommendations, amongst others. The primary cause of death for all 205 who died in the tragedy was given as 'suffocation on submersion', another term for drowning. This meant that the jury considered the horrific injuries found on some of the victims had occurred after death. The jury was also content that no one on board the *Iolaire* was under the influence of alcohol at the time of the tragedy. However, they found that the officer in charge of the vessel, Commander Richard Mason, failed to exercise sufficient caution on his approach to the harbour, and did not give orders to slow down. The *Iolaire* continued on past the harbour entrance and, with no lookout an duty as she had only half a crew on board due to holiday leave, ran onto the partly submerged rocks at speed.

Lifeboat provision on the *Iolaire* was wholly inadequate for the numbers carried that night. After all, the capacity of the *Iolaire* was meant to be 80, yet on that night she was carrying a total of 280 personnel! This fact led the jury to recommend that in future the authorities make adequate travelling arrangements for all soldiers and naval ratings.

No instructions had been given to abandon ship, but this could have been on account of all the officers and most of the crew having been killed. The panic that rose in the men was more than likely due to the fact that, without these orders, or crew members to show them how to escape, it turned out to be a case of every man for himself.

The delay in getting the life saving apparatus from the harbour to the scene was also commented upon by the jury. Drastic improvements were urged, the main point being that the apparatus should be motorised.

For the Isle of Lewis, with almost 800 of its population already having made the ultimate sacrifice in the four years of hostilities, to lose another 205 fathers, sons and brothers, in a time of peace and freedom, and in sight of their homes, was hard to comprehend.

Today in Stornoway, the victims of the *Iolaire* are still remembered. On the shore at Holm, opposite the exact site of the disaster, a small monument, dedicated to all those who perished, stands guard.

The following is taken from 'The Loss of the Royal George', a poem about a vessel that foundered off Spithead on 29 August 1782. The lines provide a fitting epitaph for the *Iolaire* disaster:

> Toll for the brave—
> The brave! That are no more:
> All sunk beneath the wave,
> Fast by their native shore.
>
> —*William Cowper*

TWICE UNLUCKY
The Sinking of the SS Rowan

On the clear autumn morning of Saturday 8 October 1921, a little packet steamer, the SS *Rowan,* sat quietly at her berth at Bridge Wharf, in the centre of Glasgow. Passengers strained to carry their luggage up the gang-planks as the overhead cranes effortlessly lifted nets full of cargo from the quay into the large holds of the vessel. Built in 1909 by D & W Henderson of Partick for the Laird Line of Glasgow, the *Rowan* was one of the largest, at 1,500 tons, and, with the ability to accommodate 200 cabin passengers, one of the best-appointed vessels that plied between the city and Ireland.

At noon she set sail, heading for her first port of call at Princes Pier, Greenock, where more passengers and cargo awaited her arrival. At Greenock, there was a delay of more than an hour as the *Rowan* awaited the arrival of the train from Glasgow, which was carrying a number of passengers intent on travelling to Ireland. The 32-member Southern Syncopated Orchestra, a group of black musicians, had finished a matineee performance at the Lyric Theatre in Glasgow and was now on its way to Dublin for its next engagement. They had missed connecting with the *Rowan* in Glasgow and were, along with some of their wives, now on the train.

At 7.20 p.m., the *Rowan* left Greenock carrying 75 passengers and 35 crew. Shortly afterwards, on passing Kildonan, she overtook a slower and much bigger ship, the 5,900 ton SS *Clan Malcolm,* which was bound for African ports. Little did anyone on board either vessel know they would meet again later that night, but in tragic circumstances.

For almost the next five hours, at her full speed of 14 knots, the

Rowan steamed south down the Firth of Clyde. The weather was fine, the sea calm and only the slightest of breezes blew. On approaching Corsewall Point at the entrance to Loch Ryan on the Wigtonshire Coast, the steamer ran into banks of floating fog. Without reducing her speed, the *Rowan* steamed on in the fog for about 15 minutes until, about 12.10 a.m., out of the mist loomed another, larger steamer, the SS *West Camak*. She was an American vessel, steaming north for Glasgow, and at 6,000 tons she was four times bigger than the *Rowan*.

There was no time for any orders to be given by the officers on the bridge of either vessel before the sharp bows of the *West Camak* struck the *Rowan* on the stern. The small vessel heeled dangerously under the blow and this was followed by the piercing screams of escaping steam coming from below her decks. At the time of the collision, almost all the passengers on board the *Rowan* had retired to their cabins for the night. Rudely awakened by the grinding crash, some got up and dressed, but the majority, clad only in night clothes, immediately ran up on deck to find out what had happened.

The *Rowan*'s captain, Daniel Brown, found that his vessel had lost all power. The propeller and rudder had been dislodged and damaged in the collision. Worse still, she had been holed below the waterline and the sea was now seeping in. The *Rowan* sat motionless and helpless in the water, slowly sinking. Captain Brown gave the order to abandon ship and as the passengers appeared from below decks, each was given a lifebelt. Others of the crew were making ready the lifeboats for launching, while the wireless operator began sending out his S.O.S. message.

Although the *Rowan* was sinking, it was doing so very slowly, almost imperceptibly. There was no panic among the passengers, as they realised they had plenty of time. They could also see that the ship that had struck them, the *West Camak*, was close by and waiting to take them on board from the lifeboats. Within ten minutes of the collision, the first lifeboat had been made ready and lowered into the calm waters. The passengers were now taking their seats in it when another ship, its lights burning brightly, steamed out of the fog. It was the *Clan Malcolm*, the ship they had passed earlier that evening just after Greenock. Any fears that the passengers on the *Rowan* had, all but disappeared at this point. Two ships were now at hand to rescue them. To most, it became nothing more than a harmless adventure on a calm night.

Those feelings lasted no more than a couple of minutes, as first one passenger, then another and another, and finally all on board the *Rowan* realised that the *Clan Malcolm* was drawing steadily nearer and nearer, with no reduction in its speed. Frantic warnings were given. Whistles were blown and sirens sounded, but to no avail. The *Clan Malcolm* continued to bear down on the small steamer until it was on top of it, slicing into the *Rowan* amidships on the port side, almost cutting her in half. The lifeboat launched from the *Rowan* had been caught between the hull of her parent ship and the bows of the *Clan Malcolm*. It was crushed and mangled beyond recognition and all the passengers in it were killed outright.

The *Rowan* began listing heavily to the starboard side. The passengers and crew knew immediately that the second collision had been the little ship's death blow and most of them began leaping over the side into the sea.

Within two minutes of being struck for the second time, the *Rowan*'s boilers blew up in a deafening explosion and this destroyed any buoyancy left in the vessel. She sank completely within seconds of the detonation. Amazingly, at the moment of sinking, the thick fog lifted, revealing a cloudless sky.

There were still a number of passengers and crew aboard the *Rowan* as she slipped below the surface, bow first. They were sucked down with her into the vortex of bubbling waters created by the sinking ship. The two large steamers quickly crewed and launched their own lifeboats and they immediately set about the task of rescuing those now fighting for their lives in the water, hanging onto anything that could float.

The Mayday call from the *Rowan* was picked up by two other ships, a Royal Navy destroyer, HMS *Wrestler* and another packet steamer, the SS *Woodcock* of the Burns Line, en route from Belfast to Glasgow. Both ships altered course and began steaming for the collision scene. HMS *Wrestler* arrived about three-quarters of an hour after the *Rowan* had sunk, but she still had a major part to play in the drama. The lifeboats of the *West Camak* and the *Clan Malcolm* had picked up a large number of survivors between them, as a result of the crews following the cries for help in the darkness. There were so many cries for assistance that the rescue crews were having difficulty in gauging where they were coming from. But once the *Wrestler* arrived on the scene, she used her powerful searchlights to illuminate the water and identify where the remaining survivors were.

The destroyer's lifeboats were also launched and their crews made many rescues. Quite a number of the Navy men ended up in the

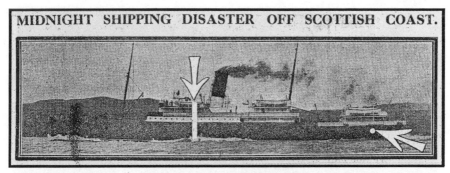

MIDNIGHT SHIPPING DISASTER OFF SCOTTISH COAST.

SS Rowan. *Circle shows point of impact with* West Camak. *Line shows collision point with* Clan Malcolm. (Daily Record)

water in an effort to help the survivors, by now exhausted, to stay afloat or to assist them into the haven of a lifeboat. Sometimes though, on reaching a lifebelt, picked out by the beam of a searchlight, they found it to be empty or to have only a piece of clothing draped over it. The person using it had slipped quietly under the waves before help had come to them.

All night long the rescue efforts continued. The searchlights constantly criss-crossed the surface of the water, occasionally picking out a lifebelt or a lifeboat, still searching for survivors. All told, the three ships involved in the rescue picked up a total of 74 survivors, 50 passengers and 24 crew. Unfortunately, two passengers rescued by HMS *Wrestler* had been so badly injured that they died almost as soon as they were taken aboard the vessel.

At dawn, and with the SS *Woodcock* having arrived too late to help with the rescue effort but now on the scene, the four vessels ringed the disaster site. Surprisingly, not one piece of wreckage from the *Rowan* was found. The three ships with survivors on board headed for Greenock. The *Wrestler* arrived first, just after 9.30 a.m., and was followed a couple of hours later by the *Clan Malcolm*. The *West Camak* arrived in the afternoon, towed by two tugs. She stopped long enough for some of her rescued to be transferred to a smaller boat for conveyance to the shore. Six survivors stayed on board the *West Camak*, as their injuries prevented them leaving the ship, and they continued on towards Glasgow, where on arrival three of them were taken to the Victoria Infirmary for treatment.

Tales of passengers who had great escapes from the disaster filled the pages of the daily newspapers for days after the event. There were stories like that of the 63-year-old stewardess of the *Rowan* who had lashed herself to broken spars from the ship in order to stay afloat, or

The SS Clan Malcolm *berthed at Glasgow. Her damaged bows are clearly visible.* (Daily Record)

of the man who caught hold of a number of deck seats, roped them together and made a makeshift raft. A number of other fellow-strugglers in the sea then held onto the raft and saved themselves from drowning. The most amazing escape story has to be that of Mr O'Reilly from Greenock. He was standing on the saloon deck of the *Rowan*, watching the *Clan Malcolm*'s approach. The large steamer ripped into the ferry almost where O'Reilly was standing and he took a flying leap at the intruding hull, managed to obtain a hold on the metal and eventually climbed up to and over the rails and onto the deck. He didn't even get his feet wet! Another piece of good fortune was experienced by Mr Ward, the regular Chief Steward on the *Rowan*. He had reported sick, needing to go into hospital for an operation, and so had missed the fatal trip. One man's good fortune is another's misfortune, and Ward's replacement, William Berridge, was counted among the dead.

Altogether, 25 passengers and 11 crew perished in the *Rowan* tragedy. Among the crew was Captain Brown, who had gone down with his ship, whilst amongst the dead passengers were 8 members of the Southern Syncopated Orchestra. The death toll would have been much higher if it were not for the fact that almost all of the

Rowan's passengers were on deck at the time of the second collision and most were wearing lifebelts. The use of the searchlights on the Navy vessel also helped to keep the number of fatalities down.

One question, concerning only the *Rowan* and the *Clan Malcolm*, was being asked over and over again. How could two ships going in the same direction be involved in a collision which resulted in such a disaster? Recriminations as to the cause of the disaster were quickly made. The owners of all three vessels involved made claims and counter-claims for damages through the civil courts. Before any decisions on these civil matters were reached, a criminal charge arising out of the tragedy was dealt with. On 27 March 1922, at Glasgow Sheriff Court, William Harris, the captain of the *Clan Malcolm*, was found guilty of operating his ship on the night of the tragedy without a wireless operator on duty. The normal procedure on a vessel of the *Clan Malcolm*'s size if the wireless operator was off duty was that a 'watcher' took his place, waiting by the radio and listening for any urgent broadcasts, like an SOS message. The wireless operator of the *Clan Malcolm* had gone off duty at 8 p.m. that night and Harris had failed to detail anyone for the job of 'watcher', leaving the radio room unattended from that time. There is no doubt that the Mayday call from the *Rowan* was received on board the *Clan Malcolm*, but there was no-one to hear it! It was the first prosecution of its kind in the country and Harris was fined £25.

In the following month, April 1922, the civil actions raised by the three owners were decided. In his judgement, Lord Anderson, sitting in the Court of Session in Edinburgh, apportioned blame for the first collision wholly on the *Rowan*, the reason being that she was steaming too fast through the fog. At the time of impact, the *West Camak* was travelling 'dead slow', at about two knots, and this is why there was so little damage done to either ship, albeit the *Rowan* had been holed below the waterline and was sinking. However, it was concluded that as the *Rowan* was sinking so slowly, once the passengers and crew were safe, she would have been salvaged and saved from a watery end.

In relation to the second collision, Lord Anderson considered the *Clan Malcolm* mainly at fault, once again for the reason that she had been travelling too fast in thick fog. He also ruled that, although the *Rowan* was sinking when the *Clan Malcolm* struck her fatal blow, there would have been enough time for all the passengers and crew to leave the packet steamer without any loss of life occurring.

Although blame for the tragedy had now been laid on those considered responsible, was it really a catalogue of negligence that resulted in the *Rowan* being in two collisions with different ships in such a short space of time? Or was the SS *Rowan* just unlucky—twice?

TRAPPED UNDERGROUND
The Redding Pit Flood

In the roll-call of tragedies that have occurred in Scotland, those involving coal mining come a close second to those that have happened at sea. Proof of this lies in the fact that in just a little under a hundred years, between 1877 and 1973, there have been 20 major incidents involving coal mines. They range from the October 1877 explosion at Blantyre Colliery in Lanarkshire that claimed the lives of 207 miners, to the May 1973 roof fall at Seafield Colliery in Fife which saw five workers killed. Any incidents since 1973 have been minor in nature, possibly due to the decline of the Scottish coal industry with the resultant widespread closure of coal mines.

Redding Colliery, about a mile outside Polmont and about four miles from Falkirk, in Stirlingshire, was not the biggest mine in the Scottish coalfields, but it was rich in coal and reserves, which made it profitable enough to employ over 70 men on every nightshift. The colliery, or to give it its full title, No.23 Pit, Redding, was located on a narrow strip of land, sandwiched between the Forth and Clyde Canal on one side and the main Glasgow to Edinburgh railway line on the other. Almost without exception, all of those employed in the mine lived in the small communities that surrounded the pit. Until that fateful day when the Redding Pit made headline news throughout the world, it had experienced only the most minor of incidents, nothing more serious than a broken bone or a cut head.

Just after 4 a.m. on Tuesday 25 September 1923, 72 miners were at work in the dark and cramped confines of the pit. They had been hard at work for the entire night and now had only a short time to go until the end of their shift.

As happens in mines, the men were not all working in the same place. They were scattered about the pit workings underground in groups of varying sizes, but the majority were at the lowest level, the coal face, which was called the Dublin Section. Without warning, an enormous tidal wave of water began rushing into the mine, and within seconds some of the miners found themselves up to their waists in ice cold water. Others were not so lucky, as in their part of the pit, the water levels rose until they almost touched the roof. Some men grabbed hold of rails that were attached to the roof in order to stop themselves being swept away by the sheer force of the torrents.

Six pitmen, who were working in one of the highest parts of the mine, managed to run clear before the waters reached them, and on reaching the surface, raised the alarm. The nightshift manager of the pit, at this time not knowing the full extent of the incident, attempted a rescue by himself. He descended the main shaft but returned very quickly as it was already deeply flooded.

One of the first orders was to send for assistance to other pits in the vicinity, and the rescue teams, or brigades as they were called, from collieries at Larbert, Auchengeich and Coatbridge responded amongst others. Two men from the colliery's own rescue team descended the main shaft to ascertain what course of action should be taken, but not before a canary in a cage and a safety lamp were lowered to check that there were no poisonous gases and there was sufficient fresh air present for humans to survive. The men were not gone very long before they reappeared with the bad news that the water in the main shaft was coming in 'like a geyser'. There was no way through in that direction.

Very soon, crowds of relatives and spectators had gathered. The news had spread by word of mouth, as, unlike an underground explosion where the noise would have been heard above, those on the surface heard or saw no evidence of this tragic event. It was calculated that the 66 men still in the pit had around 200 dependents.

Telephones were situated throughout the pit on different levels and by now, contact with some of the trapped miners had been made by this means. They were told that the main shaft was flooded and that they were to try to make their way to an old abandoned shaft, known locally as the Gutter Hole, which was about half a mile from the pithead. There they would be rescued.

The Gutter Hole shaft was not as deep as No.23 Pit, and when the rescue brigades arrived at the top of the old workings, two men were despatched into the depths to check for any pitmen. The sad news

Rescue operations being mounted at the Gutter Hole shaft. (Daily Record)

was that this shaft too was full of flood water. It had been hoped that the waters would not have reached this height. No one said anything but everyone thought that No.23 Pit was completely flooded.

The group of miners began to make their way towards the Gutter Hole, as instructed, but it was a far from easy passage. They worked at times in a frenzy, using their shovels and sometimes their bare hands in an attempt to clear a way through. They had to fight a way through torrents of ice-cold water, in some places up to their necks. It was impossible to stand up straight as nowhere in the mine was the roof ever more than five feet in height. To make matters worse, the flood waters were carrying every kind of debris and often dangerous objects could not be seen to be avoided because of the complete darkness. The half mile to the Gutter Hole became a life or death ordeal, with only luck separating those two extremes.

Among this group of pitmen fighting for survival were a father and son, Donald and Robert MacIntyre. Donald MacIntyre was the oldest of the group and he was finding that the physical exertions of the escape attempt were quickly tiring him out. After a while, he could

The sad sight of the recovery of another dead miner from the pit. (Daily Record)

take no more and he attempted to shake hands with his son as a final farewell gesture. Robert grabbed his father's hand and refused to let go, instead dragging his father through the murky waters inch by inch until they reached their goal of the Gutter Hole shaft. Once there, the men gulped at the fresh cool air. At one point, near to the end of their ordeal, they passed a fellow worker who was hanging onto the side of the tunnel and pleading to be saved. Before anyone could help him, he fell back into the fast flowing water and was swept away.

As the men clung to anything they could find, awaiting whatever was to be their fate, they noticed that the level of water was gradually falling. As it fell, a cold breeze got up. It was so cold that some of the men thought they would soon freeze to death with the combination of their wet clothes and the chill wind.

Up on the surface, rescue operations were mounted at the top of the Gutter Hole shaft. A faint shout was heard and one of the rescue team was lowered into the dark opening. The trapped men were standing waist deep in water, shouting at the tops of their voices. Then they heard a faint, but very welcome, tinkling sound. The tinkling noises were made by the thumb bells worn by all rescuers. About the size of a small bicycle bell, they gave out their distinctive signal as the rescuers worked. When they heard those bells, the miners knew they would be saved.

The crowd stood in drenching rain and watched as the rope tight-ened, indicating that the cage was now on its upward journey. The silence was eerie until the cage came into view. Two men were aboard, the rescuer carrying a trapped miner. Once safely on the surface, the miner was able to tell his rescuers that about another 20 of his col-leagues were at the bottom of the shaft awaiting rescue. The rescuers went down in the cage in ones or twos, each time arriving back on the surface with one of the entombed men, until in a very short space of time, a total of 21 men had been rescued.

Unfortunately, the last three to be brought up were found to be dead. One of those who had perished had only been married a fort-night! When the three dead miners were brought out, their bodies were laid on stretchers and canvas covers placed over them. As they were being carried to a nearby hut, the large band of relatives surged forward, vainly attempting to identify the corpses by the boots which were jutting out from under the temporary shrouds.

It had taken five hours from the time of the inrush of water before the 21 miners were rescued from the Gutter Hole. Further explora-tion of this route by the rescuers found it to be blocked, both by water and large amounts of debris. It was not going to be a route into No.23 Pit and the 42 other miners still trapped there.

It was first thought that 73 miners were in the pit when it flooded, but there were in fact only 72. One man, William Morrison, missed his shift and probably escaped death as a result.

Emergency pumps, lighting and fans were brought in. The light-ing was to enable the rescue teams to work through the night. The pumps were to clear the mine of the water and the fans to clear the pit workings of the foul and potentially fatal air condition known as 'black damp'. 'Black damp' was the name given to a deadly, poisonous and highly explosive gas, which was almost ever-present in the mines. As it was heavier than air, it would sink to the floor of the tunnels, where it lay undetected until it was disturbed by the pitmen. The rescue brigades worked continuously, pumping water out and pushing fresh air in, but still they could not make much headway in exploring the lower levels of the workings.

The source of the flood water was a mystery, but it only gave the waiting crowd a topic for speculation. One of the first rumours to circulate on the unofficial grapevine was that the nearby Forth and Clyde canal had burst and poured its contents into the underground tunnels. It was a possiblility, but was strenously denied in statements made by the owners of the pit. As the water was being pumped from

Relatives and spectators throng the site, waiting for any news of the trapped miners.
(Daily Record)

the main shaft to the surface, it was discovered that it was fresh and that it also contained live fish! The theory was that the water in the mine could have come from a loch or burn that could be miles away. Even with this information, the source could not be traced at this time.

Eventually, as the flood waters slowly receded, teams of rescuers began to search and explore the upper levels of the mine for survivors. They were hoping that some miners had reached this high ground before becoming trapped.

After three days during which the rescuers had to dig through about 130 feet of wreckage and debris, they reached the particular area they had been aiming for. This part of the mine was totally dry. No water had reached it, but no pitmen had either. Even with this setback, the rescue work continued, day after day, night after night. The crowds of relatives of the men still trapped and spectators who had gathered were silent and their spirits were sagging. As each further day passed without success, another little bit of hope for survival vanished.

By Thursday 4 October, nine days after the disaster, all hope of finding anyone alive was gone. The relatives and other spectators no longer stood around the pithead. Just after 10.30 p.m. that night, some members of one of the rescue parties working in the mine believed they could hear tapping noises. This had happened on several occasions previously, but these had been false alarms and identified as dripping water. Nonetheless, these tappings were irregular. What had raised hopes was that the tapping had become more persistent in answer to those of the rescue party. More rescuers were brought down into the mine and the digging started. All the while, as the digging was going on, clear shouts were heard coming from those who were trapped. Eventually, at about 2.30 a.m., a metal pole was forced through a rock face and the rescuers were able to speak with the trapped men. The first question was obvious. 'How many of you are there?' Back came the reply, 'Five.' More digging took place, on both sides, and within minutes, the rescuers were shaking hands and embracing those they had rescued. The first request from one of the freed miners was for a cigarette. From the 20 or so rescuers crowded into the tunnel, only one cigarette could be produced, but it was enough to satisfy the demand.

A large crowd had gathered on the surface as word of this unexpected rescue had spread. They were elated when the men appeared in the cage at the top of the Gutter Hole, but still a twinge of despair hung in the air as thoughts turned back to those 33 men still trapped below.

How had these five men survived for nine days? They had no food, apart from the first day, when they shared one slice of bread! However, they were able to drink the water that had invaded their tunnels and they had the presence of mind to force themselves to move about, crawling up and down the shaft, to avoid getting cramp. This also kept them reasonably warm. Since the day of the disaster, when they had been waist deep in water, they had remained completely dry in their place of safety.

The rescued men did not have any idea of how long they had been trapped. They thought that, at most, they had been underground for about four or five days. One of their group had been trying to measure time by gauging the growth of his beard! At one point, on realising their predicament, each of the trapped miners had written a farewell note to their families. On their rescue, they asked that these letters be destroyed without being read, a request that was readily complied with.

This success gave the rescuers renewed hope, but it was soon dashed. Word had filtered through that four more bodies had been found at this time. No matter how many pumps were brought in, and more were arriving daily from all over the UK, the water levels barely decreased. After much consultation, when no idea, reasonable or otherwise, was dismissed, a bold decision was made to take up an offer of allowing divers from Rosyth into the mine to search the water-filled tunnels for the remaining missing miners. The dangers of having their air pipes snagged or cut, or the possibility of a rockfall behind them, cutting them off from the surface, were ever present. After two days, during which the divers had ventured about 300 feet into the mine, further than any other rescue party, they came across a blockage of debris that would not allow them to progress any further. Another squad of divers, from London, had no more success than the first team. This had been the first time that divers had been used in a mine rescue operation in Scotland.

As each day passed, so any hope faded until it was gone completely. The rescue operations continued, purely in an effort to recover the bodies of the trapped miners. All through November, more bodies were recovered, almost on a daily basis, as the rescue operations explored further and deeper into the pit. On 5 December, more than two months after the disaster occurred, the body of the last miner was brought to the surface. Some of the bodies recovered were found in places where the flood waters had never reached. These miners had not died of drowning, but had succumbed to starvation and hypothermia while waiting to be rescued.

As was usual in these matters, an Inquiry into the disaster was held. It was was conducted by Sir Thomas H Mottram, His Majesty's Chief Inspector of Mines, and took place towards the end of January 1924. It lasted for nine days, during which 64 witnesses were called to give evidence and faced a total of 13,277 questions! However, the Inquiry's findings were not issued until May that year.

In evidence given to the Inquiry it was found that the water that had invaded No.23 Pit had come from old mine workings nearby. These workings, part of Redding Colliery, had been abandoned years before as the coal had dried up. Over the course of time, the old mines had filled up with water seeping in, and this eventually burst through into No.23 Pit at a point in the coal face itself or Dublin Section. Previously, No.23 Pit had a reputation for being one of the driest mines in the country. The Inquiry was told that, for a couple of weeks before the disaster, a more than usual amount of water had been pumped out of the mine on a daily basis and especially from the area of the coal face. The management of the colliery, who obviously were aware of the old mines, decided to continue removing even more coal from what was known as the 'universal dyke': the barrier between the old workings and the new pit. As it turned out, the management's plans and calculations were inaccurate and too much coal was removed, weakening the barrier. Instead of just seeping through, the water from the old mines burst through with such force it engulfed the coal-face workers in seconds and filled the remainder of the pit in minutes.

The Inquiry findings held the management of Redding Colliery to blame for the disaster on three main points. Firstly, that they made a mistake in failing to examine plans of the old workings; secondly, that they were at fault for failing to leave a substantial amount of coal on the universal dyke to act as a barrier (they were also criticised for not making test bores from the surface into the old workings to establish the location of the waters); and lastly, that the cause of the disaster was their reliance on plans and calculations that were inaccurate.

A total of 40 miners died in No.23 Pit, Redding Colliery, in what turned out not to be a unique story of disaster, but an all too familiar one: that of the management policy of profitability before all else, including the lives of the workforce.

HIT AND RUN AT SEA
The Queen Mary and the Cruiser

Some of Scotland's most terrible tragedies have occurred in time of war. As a result, a large number of these incidents had to remain secret, not only from the enemy, to save them gaining any advantage, but also from the public at large.

One little-known disaster involved a great public figure of the time, the Cunard-White Star liner, the *Queen Mary*. The story starts in December 1930 when the workforce of the shipbuilding firm of John Brown's in Clydebank began laying the keel of the next ship to be built at the yard. The vessel had no name, as yet, but was known to all involved as Contract 534. The order had been placed by Cunard Lines. It was for an ocean going liner of incredible opulence, and with an overall length of just over 1,000 feet, the vessel was to be the biggest passenger ship afloat. For the next year, work progressed steadily. By August 1931, 3,500 men were employed non-stop on the hull, which was slowly taking shape on the building ways. It was so large, it towered above the nearby tenement houses of some of the workers.

Without warning, on 12 December 1931, work on the giant vessel stopped. Contract 534 was mothballed. The dark red hull would remain on the stocks, rusting a little more each day it was exposed to the elements. For almost 2½ years, no work other than essential maintenance was done on the hull. Then as suddenly as it had stopped, work restarted in April 1934.

What had brought about this change of fortunes? The Depression had not yet ended, but as a direct result of it, Cunard Lines had reluctantly agreed to merge with another shipping line, White Star Lines. This qualified the new company for some much-needed Government

94

financial assistance, amounting to just over £2 million, which would allow not only Contract 534 to be completed, but guaranteed money for another similar ship. There was also the not so small matter of the threat now being posed by Hitler's rise to power in Nazi Germany. The Government had decided that now was the time to strengthen all of its forces, and in time of war that would include the merchant fleets.

On 26 September 1934, Contract 534 slid down the slipways and became the *Queen Mary*, although it was not until 24 March 1936 that she actually sailed away from the Clyde on her maiden voyage after being fitted out. She quickly caught the imagination of the general public, as she carried passengers around the world in unrivalled luxury. She was soon looked upon with pride by a nation eager to have some hope as the predicted war loomed closer.

When the war eventually began, it soon became clear that Britain would not be able to stand alone against the mighty German war machine. Much needed manpower, armaments and food would have to be brought into the country from overseas. The need for every and any type of sailing vessel to be pressed into service was great and the British Government commandeered most of the private fleets, including the flagship of the Cunard-White Star Line, the *Queen Mary*.

In the first week of March 1940, the *Queen Mary* was to be found berthed in New York. By the end of that week, she had been joined by her big sister, the *Queen Elizabeth*, fresh from the same Clydebank yard, having sailed the Atlantic almost straight from her launching. The *Queen Mary* had been re-painted in drab battleship grey and many of her luxurious fixtures and fittings had been removed. In their place, 5,000 bunks were fitted to accommodate the troops she had to transport. As the times required, she also had a number of guns put in place on her decks, and a sonar system fitted. This last piece of equipment was supposed to detect enemy submarines, but it turned out to be ineffective due to the noise interference generated by the liner's huge propellers as she moved through the water.

In these early days of the war, with the battlefields confined to Europe, the *Queen Mary*'s journeys were mainly between Australia and Britain, laden with ANZAC troops and equipment. After the Japanese attack on Pearl Harbor in December 1941, America entered the war and the North Atlantic convoys began carrying troops to Europe. Both the *Queen Mary* and the *Queen Elizabeth* now formed part of these convoys, due to their ability to carry large numbers of personnel. Indeed, on one voyage, the *Queen Mary* carried 16,683

The Queen Mary, *in normal livery, and in full flow.* (Daily Record)

troops and crew. This remains a record today for the largest number of people carried on a single passenger liner.

When the *Queen Mary* departed North America in convoy, usually bound for Scotland, she would be accompanied by a small group of escort ships, but for the most part she sailed alone. Once out into the open Atlantic, she left her escorts behind as she could maintain a speed of 30 knots for thousands of miles at a time, which was far superior to what other vessels were capable of. It was thought that her top speed would be her best asset in avoiding enemy attack. On approaching Scotland, another flotilla of ships assigned to protection duties would rendezvous with the *Queen Mary* and escort her safely to port.

The liner was assigned a pre-designated zig-zag course across the North Atlantic and this had to be strictly adhered to. Furthermore, her Captain was under strict instructions not to stop the vessel for any reason whatsoever. When it is considered that the great ship was carrying an average of 10,000 personnel on any one voyage, it made sense not to stop the vessel and thereby allow it become a sitting target for any waiting predator. The loss of life would have been colossal. So high was the value placed on both vessels that Hitler had given orders that any U-boat captain sinking either of them would receive a bounty of the equivalent of almost $250,000 and the Knight's Cross of the Iron

Cross with Oak Leaves, Germany's highest military honour.

On 27 September 1942, the *Queen Mary* left New York, laden with 10,398 American troops and equipment and approximately 860 crew. She was bound for Gourock. Just after midday on 2 October, after an uneventful crossing, she arrived off the southern tip of the Mull of Kintyre. This area was one of the most dangerous for any convoy. The bottleneck caused by the narrowness of the Firth at this point ensured that the location was the focus of much activity, especially by enemy submarines. As a consequence, the *Queen Mary* was still at full speed and maintaining her zig-zag course as she met up with her escort flotilla of six destroyers and a cruiser. The destroyers were assigned to protect the liner from submarine attack, while the cruiser, H.M.S. *Curacoa*, was for defence from enemy aircraft.

The Queen Mary was managing 28½ knots, while most of the rest were pushing 25 knots. Captain Boutwood of the *Curacoa* realised that at these speeds, the *Queen Mary* would soon overtake his small ship. About 12.20 p.m., he signalled the *Queen Mary* that after she had overtaken his little 4,290 ton vessel, he would follow behind her. It was the last message heard from the cruiser.

Just after 2 p.m. a number of the *Curacoa* crew began to panic. The *Queen Mary* was closer than ever before and seemed to be bearing down on the small cruiser. A few of the crewmen made for their cameras (which were banned for security reasons but carried nonetheless) for what they considered to be a 'once in a lifetime' opportunity of picturing the large liner at full speed and at close quarters. Without any further warning, the bows of the *Queen Mary* sliced into the portside of the *Curacoa*, about a third of the way along from her stern. Instead of pushing the cruiser aside, the small ship almost rolled over. On righting herself, the cruiser was immediately forced across and into the path of the bows of the huge liner. At full speed, the *Queen Mary* cut into the *Curacoa* almost at the centre point, cutting her completely in half. Even though the cruiser was armour plated, the huge bows sliced through with the greatest of ease. The boiler-room crew on the liner later reported hearing a muffled noise and assumed, wrongly, that it was caused by a larger than normal ocean wave!

Not all on board the huge vessel were unaware of what had happened. The collision had been observed from the upper levels of the liner. Many soldiers and crewmen on these decks threw as many lifejackets as they could find into the water. The Captain of the *Queen Mary*, Captain C G Illingworth, was not on the bridge at the time of the collision but arrived soon after. Remembering his strict instructions from the Ministry of War (Admiralty) not to stop his vessel for any reason, he ordered the liner to continue her journey. However, he did instruct the remaining escort ships to stay behind and assist in the rescue. Within minutes of the impact, the two halves of the *Curacoa* sank below the waves and the only noises were the shouts of the crew now fighting for their lives in the water. Debris was floating all around then, and in quite a number of places the leaked fuel from the sunken vessel had caught fire on the surface of the water. While some of the men had been trapped inside the ship and had no time to escape before both parts went under, more than half of the ship's complement of over 440 officers and ratings were now in the fiery sea.

Utter confusion reigned in the area. The escort flotilla made for the scene, but some of the vessels, unsighted by the dense smoke from the burning fuel, steamed into the middle of the debris. Their propellers churned up the ocean and, tragically, a great number of the struggling seamen, before they realised their mistake.

For nearly three hours, the rescue operations continued until the surface of the sea was cleared of men and bodies. All that remained was smouldering wreckage. From the total complement of the *Curacoa*, only 101 survivors, including the Captain, were plucked from the ocean. Almost every man rescued was covered from head to toe in black oil.

The *Queen Mary* had continued on her journey at reduced speed and arrived, without further incident, at Gourock. Although the bows of the liner had suffered severe damage, the plating had been forced inwards and had effectively sealed itself. She later was able to cross the Atlantic again in this condition to have repairs carried out in America! Prior to arriving at the Clyde port, a meeting of all officers was called on board the ship and they were instructed that nothing of the accident was to be related to anyone on landing. This order was to be relayed to the men under their command. A complete blackout on the incident was imposed.

Not until the following year, 1943, when the Admiralty started legal proceedings against Cunard for the loss of the *Curacoa*, did the general public find out about the tragedy. The total cost of the loss, including life claims, was estimated at £1,500,000. This was a massive amount of money in those days, and even more so during wartime, especially when it is considered what such a sum could have done to help the war effort.

Nothing was decided at this time. It was not until 1947, a year after the end of the war, that the Admiralty Court handed down its

The damaged bows of the Queen Mary *after cutting HMS* Curacoa *in half.*
(By courtesy of The University of Liverpool Archives)

decision, which went against the claimants. The *Curacoa* was solely to blame for the incident due to 'the negligence of those on board that vessel' including bad lookout and failing to steer clear of the *Queen Mary,* as was their duty. Unhappy with this decision, the Admiralty appealed, and in July 1947, the decision was slightly adjusted in their favour. It was now held that the *Curacoa* was only two thirds to blame and the *Queen Mary* one third. It was argued that the *Queen Mary* could have taken avoiding action which would not have incurred any greater risk of attack from enemy submarines.

This new decision cost Cunard a small fortune in compensation. But what of the truth of the incident? The *Queen Mary*, at almost 82,000 tons, completely dwarfed the 4,300 ton *Curacoa*. The incident occurred in broad daylight and in fine weather. Some reports insist that the *Curacoa* was attempting to cross the bows of the liner to investigate an 'Asdic' (sonar) sounding, possibly of a submarine. However, none of the survivors of the *Curacoa*, including the Captain, mentioned this in their statements of the time. Furthermore, there was no need for the *Curacoa*, whose role, it will be remembered, was to protect the liner from enemy aircraft, to go over to the other side of the *Queen Mary*, as at least half the vessels in the escort flotilla were already there. Amongst these vessels were destroyers which acted as the submarine hunters.

The official cause of the incident was given as 'interaction between the two vessels' and, although a little vague, it is possibly not too far from the truth. Every sailing vessel, regardless of size, creates pressure waves when moving through the water. The bigger the vessel or the faster it travels, the greater the pressure. It is highly likely that the *Curacoa*, being very close to the *Queen Mary*, got caught in the massive pressure displacement of the huge liner travelling at full speed and simply got sucked into its path, with tragic consequences. Nothing could have been done to prevent it once it had started to happen.

This was a terrible tragedy, yet a totally avoidable one. Further, and greater, loss of life occurred in many other incidents during war time, but for the *Queen Mary*, it was, without doubt, the worst in her history.

SOURCES CONSULTED

Books
Everitt, Don, *The K-Boats* (London, n.d.)
Domhallach, Tormod Calum, *Call na h-Iolair* (Stornoway, 1978)
Fisher, Joe, *The Glasgow Encyclopedia* (Edinburgh, 1994)
Harris, Paul, *Disaster!* (Runcorn, Cheshire, 1989)
Masters, David, *Wonders of Salvage* (London, 1946)
Welch, Leonard, *My Amazing Adventure: Wrecked on the Beasts of Holm* (London, 1942)
SS *Daphne: A Report* (The Glasgow Room, Mitchell Library, Glasgow)

Newspapers
Glasgow Herald
Daily Record (and *Mail*) and *Sunday Mail*
Evening Citizen
Evening Times
Scotsman
Stornoway Gazette

INDEX

SCOTTISH DISASTERS